P9-CRE-573

ALSO BY PENN JILLETTE

Sock

BY PENN JILLETTE AND MICKEY D. LYNN

How to Cheat Your Friends at Poker: The Wisdom of Dickie Richard

BY PENN JILLETTE AND TELLER

Penn & Teller's How to Play in Traffic
Penn & Teller's How to Play with Your Food
Cruel Tricks for Dear Friends

GOD, NO!

Signs You May Already Be an Atheist and Other Magical Tales

PENN JILLETTE

SIMON & SCHUSTER

New York London Toronto Sydney New Delhi

Simon & Schuster
1230 Avenue of the Americas
New York, NY 10020

First Simon & Schuster hardcover edition August 2011

For information about special discounts for bulk purchases, please contact Simon & Schuster Special Sales at 1-866-506-1949 or business@simonandschuster.com.

The Simon & Schuster Speakers Bureau can bring authors to your live event. For more information or to book an event, contact the Simon & Schuster Speakers Bureau at 1-866-248-3049 or visit our website at www.simonspeakers.com.

Designed by Joy O'Meara

Manufactured in the United States of America

1 3 5 7 9 10 8 6 4 2

Library of Congress Cataloging-in-Publication Data

Jillette, Penn.
God, no! : signs you may already be an atheist and other magical tales / Penn Jillette.
p. cm.
1. Religion—Humor. 2. Atheism—Humor. 3. American wit and humor. I. Title.
PN6231.R4J55 2011
818'.607—dc22 2010043439

ISBN 978-1-4516-1036-9
ISBN 978-1-4516-1038-3 (ebook)

· DEDICATION ·

EZ
Mox
Zz

YOU MAY ALREADY BE AN ATHEIST!

If god (however you perceive him/her/it) told you to kill your child—would you do it?

If your answer is no, in my booklet you're an atheist. There is doubt in your mind. Love and morality are more important to you than your faith.

If your answer is yes, please reconsider.

CONTENTS

Introduction:
The Humility of Loudmouth Know-it-all Asshole Atheists xiii

The Bible's First Commandment

Siegfried, Roy, Montecore, Penn, and Leather Pants 3

What's the G on the Joint? 11

King of the Ex-Jews 16

The Bible's Second Commandment

Pastor Shirley, My Mom and Dad, Lesbians, and Jesus Christ 41

Auto-Tune, Tattoos, and Big Fake Tits 48

The Bible's Third Commandment

Preach to Me and Pray for Me—Please! 59

You Are the Model? 66

Agnostics: No One Can Know for Sure but I Believe They're Full of Shit 75

The Bible's Fourth Commandment

Learning to Fly, Strip, and Vomit on a 727 83

Supreme Court Justice Ron Jeremy 95

I Also Couldn't Get Laid in a Women's Prison with a Fistful of Pardons 101

Scuba Fucking 114

The Bible's Fifth Commandment

Sister 123

Passing Down the Joy of Not Collecting Stamps 128

Up Your Santa Claus Lane 132

CONTENTS

The Bible's Sixth Commandment

Why I'm a Libertarian Nut Instead of Just a Nut 149

The Three Dogmas That Hurt Americans Most 152

Jamie Gillis: April 20, 1943–February 19, 2010 154

Penn's Bacon and a Kiss Airlines 156

The Bible's Seventh Commandment

Pitching Bullshit While in Mourning 167

The Bible's Eighth Commandment

Maybe That Thief Kreskin Will Sue Me This Time 175

Nixon the Aristocrat 183

The Bible's Ninth Commandment

In America, Noblesse Oblige Isn't Just for Noblemen 191

Would This Seem Crazy If You Read It in a Book? 195

It's Not the Heat, It's the Stupidity 199

The Bible's Tenth Commandment

You Could Be Bruce Springsteen 205

"Things Like This Don't Happen to Normal People":
The Greatest Story Ever Told 211

Hello Dere 220

Afterword:

Atheism Is the Only Real Hope Against Terrorism:
There Is No God (but Allah) 225

Acknowledgments 231

GOD, NO!

· INTRODUCTION ·

The Humility of Loudmouth Know-it-all Asshole Atheists

You don't have to be brave or a saint, a martyr, or even very smart to be an atheist. All you have to be able to say is "I don't know." I remember sitting in a room full of skeptics when I first heard Christopher Hitchens say, "Atheists don't have saints and we don't have martyrs." I'm a little afraid to put that in quotes, because no matter how brilliantly I remember any Hitchens phrase, when I go back and check, what he said was better than I remember. He is better at speaking off the top of his head after a couple of drinks than I am at remembering his brilliance later while referencing notes.

I know nothing about drinking, but I know that Hitchens did drink, and when he made that comment he was sitting next to me on the dais with a drink in front of him. But the drink was irrelevant—I could never see that it made any difference to his abilities. My doctor's brother (how's that for a source?) said there is such a thing as state-dependent learning. This explains the brilliance of all the jazz cats on heroin and how Keith Richards could play even a specially tuned guitar while as fucked-up as . . . well, Keith Richards. They're performing in the same state in which they practiced. Hank Williams was so fucked-up we don't even know which of the United States he died in. Hank's driver drove him across many state lines all night in his long white Cadillac and when they got to Oak Hill, West Virginia, Hank was dead. Hank's genius might have been state-dependent, but his dying wasn't even that.

For years it seemed Christopher Hitchens was always drunk, so he was calling up information in the same state (drunk) that he learned it (drunk). I did the Howard Stern radio show a lot in the late eighties. Many times I was on with Sam Kinison. I've never had a sip of alcohol or tried any recreational drug in my life, and I'd come in to the Stern show as rested as carny trash could be that early in the morning—focused and ready to work. Sam would come in fucked-up. *Really* fucked-up. Stern would kick off the show and Sam was always so good. I would be sweating into the mic, trying to get a clever word in here and there while in awe of how fast, insightful, profound, and motherfucking funny Sam was every second. Howard would keep us on for a long time, and at the end of the show I'd be exhausted, and Sam would just stagger out like he came in.

I used to wonder: if that was how he was in a fucked-up state, if he ever were sober, couldn't he sweep the Nobel Prizes and throw in a Fields Medal?

You don't have to be very smart, fast, or funny to be an atheist. You don't have to be well educated. Being an atheist is simply saying "I don't know."

When I was a professional dishwasher, I worked with a man named Harold. Harold sent in lyrics and the little bit of money he saved up to "song-poem" companies that advertised in the back of the *National Enquirer* and *Midnight.* He'd pay a full week's wages to have "song sharks" set his poems to music, record the songs, and try to sell them to make Harold rich. Part of the scam was to send the victim a copy of his song on a record. I now collect copies of those song-poem records. Nothing is labeled very well, and most of them are about Jesus or Nixon. I'll never know if I'm listening to a song Harold cowrote with a rip-off artist, but when I listen, I feel like I'm in touch with him. Most of the song-poems are unlistenable, but the ones that are good are heartbreaking. They are all you want in art—the cynical blasé skill of out-of-work studio musicians sight-reading hastily scribbled sheet music while a competent but bitter vocalist sings unedited, pure, white light/white heat lyrics from the heart of someone who doesn't know what the word "cynical" means. Beat that, Bruce Springsteen.

Harold was fat and ugly and sweaty. He didn't have any brainpower or hair at all, and I looked up to him. I knew other people who were a zillion times smarter than Harold, but Harold managed to show up for work, get the pots and pans clean, and deal with all the smart-assed punks, hippies, drunks, and drug users who washed dishes briefly and badly at Famous Bill's Restaurant in Greenfield, Massachusetts. Famous Bill's contained the word "famous" because they'd gotten a good review of their lobster pie in a travel magazine in the fifties. I was a hippie punk who worked with Harold for one summer and then went on with my life with Penn & Teller. Harold knew a couple little jokes, and he knew how to be polite and get to the restaurant on time and back to his apartment after work to write songs. I never talked theology with Harold—I don't know if he believed in god—but I heard him say "I don't know" about a lot of things. His smile when he admitted he didn't know was unapologetic, unless you were asking a question related to his job. If you were asking him if he liked Kerouac or Thailand, he would just say "I don't know" as a simple statement of fact. He knew very well that he didn't know.

I try to claim that I was friends with the genius Richard Feynman. He came to our show a few times and was very complimentary, and I had dinner with him a couple times, and we chatted on the phone several times. I'd call him to get quick tutoring on physics so I could pretend to read his books. No matter how much I want to brag, it's overstating it to call him a friend. I would never have called him to help me move a couch. I did, however, call him once to ask how we could score some liquid nitrogen for a Letterman spot we wanted to do. He was the only physicist I knew at the time. He explained patiently that he didn't know. He was a theoretical physicist and I needed a hands-on guy, but he'd try to find one for me. About a half hour later a physics teacher from a community college in Brooklyn called me and said, "I don't know what kind of practical joke this is, but a Nobel Prize–winning scientist just called me here at the community college, gave me this number, and told me to call Penn of Penn & Teller to help with a Letterman appearance."

I guess that's close to a friend.

My friend Richard Feynman said "I don't know." I heard him say it several times. He said it just like Harold, a simple statement of fact. When Richard didn't know, he often worked harder than anyone else to find out, but while he didn't know, he said "I don't know."

I like to think I fit in somewhere between my friends Harold and Richard. I don't know. I try to remember to say "I don't know" just the way they both did, as a simple statement of fact. It doesn't always work. It seems that with "climate change" we're all supposed to know, but I'll get to that later in the book.

One attack I've heard theists make against atheists is, "So, you atheists think you know everything? You think you're smart enough to know everything? You think science can figure out everything? There are more things in heaven and earth, Horatio, than are dreamt . . ." That quote is from my good friend Mr. Straw Man, but it's an idea we hear all the time: atheists are arrogant and don't think they need god, because they've got it all figured out. I think people who make that accusation are confusing style with content. I'm a loud, aggressive, strident, outspoken atheist, and I'm an asshole—but what I'm claiming is not in any way arrogant. It couldn't be more humble. It's just "I don't know."

I don't know how the world was created. I don't know how humans got here. There are lots of good guesses, and we keep testing those guesses trying to find where they're wrong. Science has helped a lot, but we don't know. And maybe we never will. I mean, we, all of us, the people alive right now, will certainly never know, but it seems almost as likely that no humans will ever know. How could we? We will keep getting closer, we will keep knowing more and more. I guess string theory might explain some things, but I don't know. I don't understand jack shit about string theory. Evolution explains a lot. I think I get a little bit about that. Evolution really does seem to make a zillion pieces fall into place. It's the answer to a lot of questions that, before Darwin, had to be answered with "I don't know." The theory of evolution keeps, you know, evolving—it keeps changing. Now, we do know a lot, but the number of "I don't know"s is still infinite. Aren't there a few different kinds of infinity? I don't fucking know. I sure can't picture infinity. What does it mean to go on forever? I don't know. That's how Harold's coworker Penn, the dishwasher, would say it—a simple statement of fact: "I don't know."

Where is the humility in being a theist? There is none. What would it mean for me to believe in god? It would mean that I know. Not just that I might happen to know about Kerouac, Thailand, liquid nitrogen, and vector calculus identities, but that I know that there is an omniscient, omnipotent, omnipresent power in the universe that I can't prove to you, but that I know because I have faith. I know because I say I know. I can feel it. I would maybe have faith that this force in the universe is for good. Maybe it's tied in with love. Maybe I know that this force in the universe will give everlasting life and cares very much where I stick my fucking cock. Maybe I would know that there is a supreme power in the universe and that supreme power cares about me. Not everyone who believes in god believes all of those things. But it doesn't matter—whatever they say god is, they're saying they know. There is no humility. They believe because they say they believe. Some people who believe in god distort the meaning to the point where . . . well, even I could say I believe in god. Some will tell you "God is love" and then defy you not to believe in love. But, if X = Y, why have a fucking X? Just keep it at Y. Why call love god? Why not call love . . . love? "Beauty is god." Okay. If you change what the word means, you can get me to say I believe in it. Say "God is bacon" or "God is tits" and I'll love and praise god, but you're just changing the word, not the idea. Some think that god will answer prayers. They think that their prayer can influence the behavior of an omnipotent, omniscient power. How do you figure that? How come it's rare to see people on TV saying that god made them lose the stupid ball game or killed that baby in the house fire? How come every time someone says that god told them to kill their whole family, the religious people say right away that the faithful murderer was crazy? You never see religious people saying "I wonder if that murder was a miracle. I wonder if god is speaking to us directly again."

Maybe they really don't believe this shit either.

I could scream at the altar of a church, with a crucifix stuck deep up my asshole, that I fuck Jesus Christ hard through the hand holes and cream on his crown of thorns, and I will never hit the level of blasphemy that's required for someone to pray to god for their family's pet dog to return home. The idea that someone can claim that they know there's a god because they feel it, because they trust a book that they were raised with, because they had an epiphany, and then ask this god to change its mind about its plan for the universe is arrogant. Once you say you have the answer to everything, but you can't prove it to anyone else, I don't think you can accuse anyone else of being arrogant. I think you are the king of kings of the arrogant assholes.

And "I don't know" doesn't mean "There might be a god." That's the different kind of "I don't know," that's not Harold and Richard's honest, humble "I don't know." Being an atheist means you don't believe in god. When someone asks if god exists and you humbly say "I don't know," you've answered the question honestly. Once you've answered "I don't know" to the existence of a god, the answer to whether you *believe* in god pretty much has to be no. That doesn't mean you're saying it's impossible for there to be a god, or that we couldn't have evidence of a god in the future. It just means that right now you don't know. And if you don't know, you can't believe. Believing cannot rise out of "I don't know."

Is there an elephant in your bathtub right now? If you humbly answer "I don't know," then when asked if you believe there's an elephant in your bathtub right now, the answer would be no. Anything is possible, but there's no reason to believe it until there's some evidence. Once you're an atheist, anything is possible. You are leaving open the possibility of Jesus Christ as lord, and Thor, and invisible gremlins living in your toaster. It's all possible, but . . . I don't know. And until I know—until there's some evidence—I'm an atheist.

What could be humbler than that? You don't have to be smart or well educated, you just need to be humble. And if you're a libertarian atheist, there can be no commandments. There can be no edicts. It's all down to the individual. No one knows what's best for other people. I don't even know what's best for myself.

I was asked by Glenn Beck to entertain the idea of an atheist Ten Commandments. It was his rhetorical exercise to try to force the incorrect point that the biblical Ten Commandments were just common sense. Even though my heroes Hitchens and George Carlin have taken a pass at the Ten Commandments, I wanted to do my own. I wanted to see how many of the ideas that many people think are handed down from god really make sense to someone who says "I don't know."

Borscht Belt comics and a lot of web pages have used the gag "The Ten Suggestions." All joking aside, that seems like the right feeling. This book is just some thoughts from someone who doesn't know. I've tried to throw in a couple of funny stories, and there's a lot of rambling. Some of the stories have nothing to do with atheism directly, but they will give you a feel for how one goofy atheist lives his life in turn-of-the-century America. If you're still claiming that you're religious, you can compare and contrast. I think you'll find that I'm just like you, if you're the kind of guy or gal who's dropped his or her cock into a blow-dryer. Try to remember, when it all comes down, I just don't know.

But . . . god? No! There is no fucking god!

The Bible's First Commandment

Thou shalt have no other gods before me.

The greatest thing about provable reality is that by definition reality is shared. Every argument is really an agreement—an agreement that there is a reality that can be shared, judged, and discussed. To argue over whether the speed of light is constant or Batman could beat up the Lone Ranger is to share the parameters. God is solipsistic; reality is shared.

ONE ATHEIST'S FIRST SUGGESTION

The highest ideals are human intelligence, creativity, and love. Respect these above all.

Siegfried, Roy, Montecore, Penn, and Leather Pants

I loved the Siegfried and Roy show at the Mirage in Las Vegas, Nevada. I just loved it. It made me cry. It filled my heart with joy. It made me proud to be in show business. The magic in the show sucked. I don't like seeing animals onstage. I couldn't follow the plot of the show. The Michael Jackson song written for the show was bombastic, saccharine, and plain nonsense. I didn't care about the staging, choreography, costumes, or lighting.

I liked nothing about the Siegfried and Roy show—but I loved all of it. I loved it with all my heart. I saw it several times, and every time it inspired me and filled me with a rage to live. Bob Dylan said, "Art is the perpetual motion of illusion. The highest purpose of art is to inspire. What else can you do? What else can you do for anyone but inspire them?"

Siegfried and Roy always inspired me. They showed me how pure and simple art could be. Their show had a zillion dancers and big stupid props. Their show was dripping with over-the-top hype and empty glitz, and had more honesty, purity, and bravery than all the alternative folk lo-fi acts at all the non-Starbucks coffee shops in the state of

Washington put together. I've quoted, since I was a child, Lenny Bruce saying the purpose of art is to stand naked onstage. I can't find that quote by Lenny in any books, records, or transcripts. I think I made it up. So . . .

The purpose of art is to stand naked onstage.

—Penn Jillette

Too bad it's a quote from an asshole and not a genius, but it's still true. Lenny Bruce, playing a strip club before he made it, once came out onstage wearing nothing but a bow tie and a pair of shoes. He stood onstage and pissed in a knothole in the floor to protest the danger of that stage knothole to the strippers in high heels. Teller and I used to strip naked onstage to prove there was nothing up our sleeves. But Lenny Bruce, Penn Jillette, and Teller were never as naked onstage as Siegfried Fischbacher and Roy Horn. Siegfried and Roy would walk onstage to huge applause (beefed up by prerecorded applause over the loudspeakers) in their goofy, sparkly, rhinestone-skin coats and leather pants with codpieces. Their hair would be perfectly frosted and layered and they'd be wearing almost as much makeup as Bill Maher. They looked out at their audience, and we could all see deep into their hearts. They were completely naked onstage. So naked you could see into their past: the twelve-year-olds in Germany standing in front of their mirrors, maybe each with his cock and balls tucked between his legs hiding, arms up in the air like the pope, smiling big toothy smiles, hearing this applause in their heads. It was all pretend when they were children, and as adults it was all real. So painfully, embarrassingly, proudly, honestly, purely real. The tricks didn't matter, the animals didn't matter, the shithouse rat–crazy King of Pop grunting about mystical gardens, violets, devotions, and hallucinations didn't matter. Nothing mattered but the raw, desperate purity in the eyes of Siegfried and Roy looking out at the crowd. They wanted to be onstage so much—too much—that I was proud to be just an extra in their fantasy. I applauded, screamed, and cried my eyes out. I loved Siegfried and Roy onstage.

I also loved Siegfried and Roy backstage.

When P & T went to see S & R, we went backstage. If you go backstage at the Penn & Teller Theater, it's not glamorous. We've got very plain dressing rooms. We each have our desk and computer—those are the centerpiece of each room—and we're usually typing right up until we go on. I have music playing and a left-wing or right-wing television news station with no sound on. I read the closed captions when I look up from my computer. Teller is forced to hear my shuffled 650 gigs of nut music through the shared beige wall. Teller has a poster up for the production of *Macbeth* he directed and some paintings by his mom and dad. I have a big poster of D. A. Pennebaker's Bob Dylan documentary *Don't Look Back,* some Ayn Rand handwritten pages from *Atlas Shrugged,* an eight-by-ten of Raymond Burr and the rest of the cast of *Perry Mason,* some Tiny Tim pictures, and artwork by and pictures of my children.

Our greenroom is the Monkey Room. It's a jungle-themed room with smoking monkeys and a small fridge with Blenheim really spicy ginger ale. There are a few pictures on the wall of us with people like Madonna, Warhol, Steve Martin, Run-DMC, Iggy Pop, and David Allan Coe. Most of the decorating was done by the TV show *While You Were Out.* If not for that TV show, our greenroom wouldn't even be green, it would be hotel beige with an off-white acoustic-tile ceiling. The fluorescent light fixtures show shadows of dead roaches. The Rio All-Suite Hotel and Casino is very clean, so they're probably made of rubber and put there by Teller. I won't give him the satisfaction of asking.

Backstage at Siegfried and Roy was real showbiz. It was as pure as their walking onstage. Roy had a huge jungle-themed bedroom. We have pictures of monkeys backstage; Roy had real live wild animals in cages all around the room. He needed a live ocelot, a snake, and a few birds in his bedroom so he could commune with them before the show. We surf porn on our computers. Roy meditates with endangered species. Everything was opulent, that golden-toilet, Dubai kind of opulent, that poor-no-more Elvis opulent. S & R didn't greet us backstage barefoot in jeans and T-shirts like P & T, wolfing down after-show room service on

TV trays; they came out in yak-hair dressing gowns. Teller and I don't even shower after the show, we just throw our street clothes on over the sweat. S & R were showered, their hair was blow-dried, they smelled pretty, and they were wearing makeup. They were wearing makeup backstage after the show and after showers. Penn & Teller don't even wear makeup onstage. S & R looked better backstage after their show than P & T looked onstage at the Emmys. They are fucking superstars; we are fucking pigs.

Teller and I sat at S & R's backstage bar with the Masters of the Impossible themselves. Siegfried kissed my date's hand and showed her a card trick that had the punch line built into a fancy wooden clock in the wall. The clock bloomed with flowers and her freely selected card. They had a . . . what's the word? "Assistant" isn't right. Butlers don't have their heads shaved and a coolie topknot. Valets are obsequious but don't bow and cast their eyes down. I guess this guy was a servant. A very old-school servant. Like Dark Ages–school servant. I don't know what he was, but he waited on Siegfried and Roy, and he seemed thrilled about it. I don't mean he got them a Coke from the fridge. He would put cigarettes in their mouths and light them. Really. I was nervous. I didn't fit into this kind of showbiz. Not at all. Fischbacher and Horn's childhoods in Germany were probably humbler than my dead-factory hometown in Massachusetts, but they had risen above their past and I was still living mine. I was dressed for the dishwashing job I would have kept had I stayed in Greenfield: work shirt and dirty jeans. They were dressed for the jobs they were destined for. They are superstars. I fiddled with a cigarette on the bar and their . . . servant ("servant" really doesn't bring up the full image) brought me a brand-new pack, opened, with a cigarette sticking out ready for me. He would have lit it for me too. If I'd wanted, he'd probably have expertly massaged my chest to suck the smoke in.

S & R & P & T talked. We have a lot in common. All four of us are part of a showbiz duo. Put Tommy and Dick Smothers, Mick Jagger and Keith Richards, and Trey Parker and Matt Stone in that room with us, and we would have all understood everything. Tolstoy had it right: successful partnerships are all the same. Unsuccessful ones are all different. Sam, Dave, Phil, Don, Simon, Garfunkel, Lennon, McCartney, Gilbert, and Sullivan all went their separate ways in separate ways. Dino Martin left Jerry Lewis for different reasons than Cher left Sonny, but I work with Teller for all the same reasons Abbott stayed with Costello.

When I was on Howard Stern all the time, I spent some time trashing Siegfried and Roy. I don't do gay jokes, but the stuff I did about them fucking the tigers was close enough to be cruel and outside of my comfort range. The Stern show was intense, and I was out of my league. But the show was important—it sold more tickets than anything else we did. I pushed hard. I was scared and I would say anything to try to please Howard, so I sometimes went too far. There are things I still wince about. I lost a few friends and a couple of girlfriends from nonsense I spewed on that show, but when I trashed S & R in public there was often a voice mail from Siegfried the day after thanking me for the mention. He wasn't being sarcastic, it was just a thank-you because I'd mentioned them. S & R are classy showbiz all the way. They took the high road, even when I hadn't.

Siegfried and Roy invented the big Vegas magic show. I'm not sure there would be a Penn & Teller Theater in Las Vegas if not for our glittery Teutonic brothers. Before S & R all magic shows were just, as J. D. Salinger wrote, "all that David Copperfield crap." Everyone just toured. Only variety shows and lounge acts stayed in Vegas full-time. Those are just the business changes Fischbacher and Horn made; S & R did big artistic changes too. As surely as Miles Davis invented a few forms of music, S & R were the birth of the cool animal act in magic. As a result, Penn & Teller have to explain why we *don't* have sexy dangerous animals in our show (we have only a cow). People think all magicians have wild animals in their shows, and many of them do now, but that's all Fischbacher and Horn. Houdini vanished an elephant, and some guys did horses or mules, and there were always rabbits and birds, but Siegfried and Roy upped the ante with tigers and shit. They created the act that most magicians are ripping off now.

Siegfried and Roy did more than just combine a big illusion

show with a big animal show to make a big Vegas show. Roy also changed the way dangerous animal acts were done. From Frank Buck to Gunther Gebel-Williams, animal trainers made it look dangerous and hard. I started out as a juggler, and the whole idea was to make everything look as hard as possible. Teller and I end our show by ostensibly catching bullets in our teeth. It's way way safe, and we hope the audience knows it's safe, but it feels way way dangerous. We don't get too cheesy with it, we don't do that David Blaine/Criss Angel life-and-death shit, but we still make sure people think about the guns as dangerous items. Lion tamers always had whips and chairs and they were in a cage with dangerous beasts. They were in there with things genetically programmed to kill them. That was the entertainment. It was big swinging-dick macho that your tiger could get your tiny human swinging dick caught between his huge tiger fucking teeth. Animal trainers would crack the whip and put their heads in the lion's rotten-meat-stinking (that's one word in German) mouth. Roy didn't do it that way. He did this crazy nutty insane stupid thing where he took something really really really dangerous and made it look like love. No whips, no chairs, no dominating the beasts. He treated them like his friends. He loved them. The amazing part was that it was impossible to get your little pussy to do that at home—how did he get those big, fluffy, beautiful, cuddly tigers to do it?

When you take something easy and safe and make it look difficult and death-defying, you are a cheesy circus act. When you take something impossible and make it look easy, you're an artist. It's always back to Miles Davis and Picasso, and let's throw in David Letterman. What they do looks easy and simple and, well, it just happens to be close to impossible and stirs your heart to the very depths. That's the way Roy played the tigers. It made me crazy. I fucking hate big dangerous animals. I hate them. When I was at Ringling Brothers and Barnum & Bailey, the Greatest Show on Earth, the animal guys would walk these fucking big smelly monsters on leashes around the ring while I was practicing my juggling and it just made me tremble. I would sneak off and lock myself in a room. I've ridden elephants and they scare me shitless. They could kill me on a whim. Every species of living thing has individuals who go crazy and there's no way of telling which ones they are. I might be riding on an eight-ton gray Ted Bundy with a trunk. But Roy really believed those eating machines loved him. I don't want to see animals onstage, I don't think show business should ever be really dangerous, but he invented a new art form, no doubt about it. I was always so worried about him.

When you're a headliner in Vegas there are press events where you have to show up to prove you're working. That meant we would see S & R on red carpets and at charity events. They would walk the red carpet like royalty, and I would limp and lumber down the red carpet like a New England shit-kicking farmer in my work boots. It didn't matter how many S & R tiger-fucking jokes I'd made the week before on Stern—S & R greeted us with big toothy smiles and real joy in their hearts. We'd stand there chatting while cameras flashed, Siegfried and Roy in glitter tuxes or paisley Nehru jackets with perfectly tailored tight leather pants, and Penn in an off-the-rack shirt from a big and tall men's store and maybe an indifferent suit jacket. They were superstars. I was there to sell someone a car. I tried to pass it off that I was being all humble and shit, but the truth is, I was the one who was being self-aggrandizing. I was acting like just showing up was enough to make people happy. Siegfried and Roy were doing their jobs and I was slouching and slacking. The audience doesn't pay us these stupid amounts of money so we can invest wisely or even help people with Kiva, they pay us that money so we'll do stupid shit. So we'll show up in a Rolls-Royce with a driver in a little hat and we'll all be wearing leather pants. Even faced with my self-absorbed, unprofessional clothing, knowing I'd be trashing them on any radio show I hadn't properly prepared for, they would be smiling at me, hugging me, really happy to see me. We would pose for pictures together, two superstars and a guy who was there to clean up after the party was over. Their smiles were big, toothy, and radiant, and mine looked like I had just farted.

Then Roy got his fucking head bit off. We had just finished our show and we came backstage and were told that Roy had an accident.

"Accident" is an odd word when you've intentionally gotten close to a predator, but Teller and I rushed over to the hospital, where we ran into Lance Burton and every other magician in town. Bernie, S & R's perfect manager, is exactly the guy they should have. He is as purely a manager as S & R are purely superstars. Bernie asked me if I'd go on camera and give updates as to how Roy was doing. I was going to talk about S & R from my heart and not do jokes. I was there at the hospital most of the night. I was there the next day. Here I was, the host of a show called *Bullshit!,* listening to all the stories about the tiger really trying to save Roy's life and not rolling my eyes. This here atheist was at the candlelight vigil. This here atheist stood quietly while people publicly prayed.

I don't believe Montecore the tiger was trying to help Roy. I believe Montecore was trying to bite Roy's fucking head off. Roy protected Montecore after the "accident." Roy still cares for Montecore. I don't believe the praying helped Roy at all. I believe it was a team of medical professionals working their asses off that kept Roy's head on. But I didn't say any of that that night.

A couple of days after the accident, I went to the Forum Shops at Caesars. There's a Versace store there. I had never been in it. I went in and I spent a few thousand dollars (yup, a few *thousand* dollars) on a pair of tight leather pants. Really tight, like I was wearing a codpiece. I put on a flashy shirt and ran a brush through my hair. I tried to walk in my leather pants, not like a farmer, but like a star.

"Mind Is the Magic"

—Michael Jackson

What's the G on the Joint?

"What's the G on the joint?" is carny slang for "How do you do the scam?" "G" probably stands for "gaff," and the gaff is the secret of the trick. I've heard some guys say "affis/gaffis" but that's too affected even for me.

Teller and I spent an afternoon in a hotel room at a magic convention arguing with David Blaine about the use of the word "trick." He hates the word. Just hates it. He thinks it takes the magic out of magic. We love the word. Just love it. We think it takes the magic out of magic. He thinks that a trick is supposed to be something mystical, which I guess I agree with; everything mystical is just a trick.

It's always astonished me how any magician can be spiritual. There are hippie magicians who do drum circles in the woods and then do a card force and a false shuffle and think they're expressing something real. "Imagine a universe so limitless and yet so all-connected that you chose the three of clubs!" There are even "gospel magicians" who'll do a cheesy "cake in the hat" trick and tie it to the resurrection of zombie Christ: "And god so loved the world that he gave his only son our lord and savior to die for our sins and give us this chocolate cupcake out of your baseball hat!" It seems like depicting the most important event in one's philosophy with a $19.95 trick from a joke shop cheapens it a bit. Again, I guess I agree completely.

I think "trick" is a noble human word. It's something you learn. It's something you teach a monkey to do. That all seems good to me. I'm proud to do tricks. I'm proud of using gaffs. After a few hours of arguing with David and his posse we walked together to the elevator. There's a thing with pro magicians: we don't ask each other how the tricks are done. Some of it is politeness, not putting a person in a position where they have to say "I won't tell you," and some of it is a big swinging dick—if you don't ask them, they don't know you don't know. Real classy old-timers would say, "You really baffled me with that trick, maybe you'll let me in on it someday."

I've never said that. Fuck you and your stupid trick, I don't care.

On the walk to the elevator David took Teller and me aside, separately, and confided in us that the hunger thing he did in England was "real." When he was doing the starving trick in that Plexi box by the Tower Bridge in London in 2003 for forty-four days, he claimed he was really hungry for a long time. I'm not a cynic, I'm a skeptic—I try to question information but not motives. But when it comes to David Blaine, I question motives.

Before David took me aside, and I saw him take Teller aside, it never crossed my mind to ask if David had been really starving in the box. I took it like I take most tricks, for the ideas, and I found these particular ideas repulsive.

In the bullet trick in our show, Teller and I point real guns in each other's real faces and pull the real trigger. It's a horrific image, but at the end, we're fine. That's the beauty of the trick—we're okay at the end. Lots of people get guns fired into their faces, but they're not okay after. In the fantasy of theater, we conquer the pain, suffering, and death.

When Paul McCartney went to see David Blaine starving in the box over the Thames, Sir Paul called him "this stupid cunt." David wasn't getting fatter in the box. Fatter without food could be a good trick. Blaine was hungry in the box, and being hungry when one doesn't eat isn't a good trick. It isn't a trick at all. There are people all over the world doing this hunger trick against their will, so who cares about the cunt in the box? In 1981 Bobby Sands starved himself to death in prison in an attempt to get the English government to treat IRA members in jail as political prisoners. Bobby Sands got emaciated and died for a cause he believed in. David Blaine got publicity with mocking children throwing food at him and getting called a cunt by the cute Beatle. Getting called a cunt by the Sir Beatle is the only part I thought was pretty boss.

David was getting fed water while he was cunting in the box, and the water could have had glucose in it, I suppose. If Teller and I were doing it, we wouldn't have been happy with a little sugar water; we would have been sneaking in steak dinners and Twinkies and getting fat. I don't know how my getting fat is a good trick, I do it all the time, but getting fat while starving would at least be unexpected. It would be wish fulfillment for starving people.

I was so busy thinking about what a shitty trick it was that I didn't think much about the gaff. The instant that David took me aside, put a hand on my shoulder, made eye contact, and told me and then Teller, with utmost sincerity, that he'd really been starving himself, I knew there was a G on the joint. Why talk to both me and Teller if you're not going to lie to us? But it doesn't matter. If you ask whether he "did it for real or not," you're missing the point.

David Blaine and Criss Angel did an odd thing. They became famous as magicians and then claimed to be doing things for real. Criss did a lot of sit-ups and then stuck fishhooks in his tits and wanted people to know he was really doing it. "You know, the steamroller thing and the card tricks were lies, but the fishhooks in my tits, why would I lie about that?"

I started out as a juggler, and jugglers do things for real. There are some juggling tricks that are gaffed, but no juggler I know is comfortable using them. Jugglers like to tell the truth. I do things in the Penn & Teller show that are for real and I do stuff where I'm lying my ass off, and the audience knows the difference. I want them to be able to tell the difference. I like the audience to know when I'm telling the truth and when I'm lying. But David and Criss went into this area that wasn't juggling and wasn't magic. Some of their stuff was the kind of thing that morning DJs used to do ("I'll do four days on the air with no sleep and *no disco*!"), and before DJs, flagpole sitters. David Blaine even did one gag that was exactly flagpole sitting. The only idea of these stunts is desperation.

Before David did his "buried alive" gag in NYC, his people called Teller and me and asked if we could help with the trick. We were taking a break around that time and some of our crew guys went to NYC to help build a box for David Blaine to lie in and shit all over himself. Our crew assumed they'd be sneaking him out of the box, but David wanted to really stay in the box doing nothing and living in his own stink. This is how he got to be a star. If doing nothing for over a week is the mark of a superstar, my brother-in-law should be Elvis Gaga. The hard part of David's stunt was keeping the press far enough away from him when he got out of the box that they wouldn't gag from his smell. Being marinated in your own buried personal Porta Potty for a week is not sexy.

David is a magician who did card tricks and camera tricks, and now he wants his stunts to be taken as real. But "real" doesn't mean anything in this context. Even if there's no G on the joint, even if he "really does it," he's still not really doing it. It's still showbiz and not science. "Do you think David Blaine really held his breath that long on *Oprah*?" I don't care. I don't want the question asked.

A magic trick has to be good enough as a magic trick that when you know there's a G on it, it's still interesting. It still needs to mean something. I love people who have passion and obsession. I love that there are crazy sons of bitches who want to do free diving and go as long as they can without air just to see if they can do it. I love that pure obsession. But I don't care about dilettantes on *Oprah*. Once there are lights all over, and hype and hoopla, it's no longer science to me. It's no longer humanity.

When David pops up in the silver wetsuit with the queen of daytime TV looking amazed, it is by definition a trick. It's a stunt—and to ask if he really did it is to not understand that art is supposed to be different from reality. And that's the cool part about art.

These are all artistic differences, not moral differences. David is a very good person. I like him. We're not close, but I consider him a friend. The next time I see David, I wonder if he'll walk me to the elevator, put his hands on my shoulders, look me in the eye, and say, "I really wasn't breathing, bro."

That'll prove it.

"Too Many People"

—Paul McCartney

King of the Ex-Jews

After every show, Teller and I meet the audience. We stand in the lobby and talk to anyone who wants to talk to us about anything. We are happy to sign autographs, but that's not why we're out there. It's really just habit. When we started out, at fairs, renaissance festivals, and little shit hole theaters, there was either no backstage or the backstage was so unpleasant it was better to be out with the audience. No one wanted our autographs, but some people wanted to talk to us, and we'd chat.

We continued to meet the audience Off-Broadway, and then, when it was time to go to Broadway, some thought we would stop hanging out, but we didn't. We don't really know how to sit backstage after a show. We relax and come down by talking to the folks who just watched our show.

We still play places that are small enough that we can meet everyone who would want to talk to us in an hour or so, and what the fuck else have we got to do? Since it's over a thousand people, and we've been controversial now and again on TV, we now have security guards near us, and they're ready to protect us from anyone who would want to hurt us, but what they really do is tell people where the restrooms are.

Meeting our audiences, or at least the members of the audience who would like to meet us, makes us different from other entertainers. We aren't scared of our audiences. We've learned that the crowds that other entertainers might hate—the quiet crowds—include many people who are loving the show. I love quiet crowds now; I don't see them as lacking enthusiasm, I see them as paying attention.

We've learned that a joke that didn't get a loud laugh might be someone's favorite line. I've learned that even when you're the first clumsy motherfucker thrown off *Dancing with the Stars,* you might still have connected in an honest way with some people in that huge faceless TV audience. Teller usually has a few spoken lines in every show, but people like to consider him silent. They like to play it that way. We don't have to pretend that Teller never talks. It's just a show and we know it and they know it. After the show Teller talks to anyone who might want to talk to him. An audience member will chat with Teller for a few minutes, but when that audience member gets back home, he'll explain to his friends that Teller never talks. We're all in the show together.

I've been known to go out to eat with people I meet after the show, and I have lifelong friends whom I first met in conversation after the show.

One magical night after the show, the reason I got into show business paid off. An attractive woman waited around until everyone else was gone and told me she'd seen an advance DVD of the first few shows of the first season of *Bullshit!* at a Skeptics Society meeting. She was very complimentary and said she'd been talking about our show with the Amazing Randi and Richard Dawkins. Randi is my mentor, and Dawkins is an idol of mine whom, at the time, I'd never met. She chatted me up a little more and invited me out for coffee.

It's coming up on ten years later and now I'm that fan-girl's husband, and we have two wonderful children together. I'm not afraid of stalkers; I married one.

One night after the show a man in his thirties came over and asked me for an autograph. As I signed his copy of my novel, *Sock,* he told me that he had been an Orthodox Jew, and now he was an atheist and he wanted to thank me for helping him make that change. He said that listening to my radio show had had a very big effect on him. He was considerate and didn't want to monopolize my time when others were waiting for me, so he didn't say much more, just took his autograph and left.

When the crowd had cleared out, he was hovering. He was waiting like guys who want me to do a quick video ID for their podcast, women who want me to sign a breast or two, and weasels who want to ask me to do a show or a charity event that our manager turned down.

This ex-Orthodox ex-Jew was waiting for me where my future wife had stood to ask me out. He was polite and nervous as he told his story. I'm not going to write his name. As you read on, you'll understand why he wouldn't want it published. You wouldn't believe his name anyway; it's a joke Jewish name and you'd think I made it up, so I will make it up. I'll call him Atheist Boy, or AB for short.

AB was a freshly born atheist. His family were all still Orthodox. He had a lucrative job at a big retail company and many of the people he worked with, as well as his bosses, were Orthodox Jews.

I hadn't given him the doubts in his religion, nor had I given him any theology, but somehow, listening to my radio show had given him some sort of inspiration to say he was an atheist. I have no idea how I'd had this kind of effect on him. I'm from Goyfield, Massachusetts. We had two students in our whole high school class who took the Jewish days off from school. The father of one of those children owned the Howard Johnson where I washed dishes (I also washed dishes at the Franklin County Public Hospital, as well as Famous Bill's Restaurant—I got around), and I'd had some contact with him, but just as a rich guy, not as a person. My cohost on my radio show was Michael Goudeau, and he's a coon-ass from Louisiana. We were about as culturally non-Jewish as we could be. I've been told that the definition of *goyishe kop* (non-Jew thinking) is buying a boat. Goudeau and I, together, are a big old leaky cigarette boat. We both knew our Lenny Bruce and the Yiddish of the comedy business, but we sure weren't anything for an ex-Orthodox Jew to identify with.

I thanked AB and started to walk away, but he had more to say. He had spent his whole life kosher, he said. He'd never eaten pork, or bacon, or shellfish. No milk and meat together. Never. He had flown out to Vegas on business and was taking some extra time to see our show and to think about his theology. On the plane they had offered a lousy microwaved cheeseburger but he couldn't bring himself to eat it. He couldn't do it. Here he paused. I've gotten laid after my shows. I met my wife after a show. I know about forced awkward preintimacy.

(Before this tale gets all heavy and touching and shit, I would like to give you the best pickup line anyone ever used on me after a show. Yes, my wife praising *Bullshit!* and dropping "Randi" and "Dawkins" was great and it worked, but, with all love and respect to my wife, another woman creamed her on the immediate sexual pickup front. Remember, this is the Penn & Teller Show, and I'm Penn. I say "My name is Penn Jillette and this is my partner Teller" as the first and last line of every show. And behind me while I'm in the lobby after the show, there are big pictures of me with my name in huge block letters right over my head. After one show I was out in the lobby talking and signing autographs, and a woman hung back and waited for people to clear out. When they were gone, she walked over, cocked her head at a questioning angle, and said very clearly and directly, "Fuck me if I'm wrong, but is your name Debbie?")

All the sexual pickups I've heard were much less intimate and vulnerable than what AB was about to say. He quietly asked me if he could eat his first non-kosher food with me. He wanted me to join him for a bacon cheeseburger. He said it would mean a lot to him. That's a lot harder to say than "fuck me." I was so moved. I didn't know what to say. I still don't know how to describe the feeling. I was certainly honored. I certainly felt unworthy. But it was more than that. I invited him backstage and said, "Yeah, c'mon back, meet the guys, and we'll watch you eat."

I walked him back and left him in the Monkey Room with Jonesy, the monster jazz piano player in our show, while I changed my clothes. By the time I got back to AB, Teller was in the Monkey Room, along with a friend of ours from the MIT Media Lab who had come backstage after seeing the show. Zeke was also there. Zeke is one of the guys who sets up all the magic for us. There are places in the show where our lives are in Zeke's hands. He's the youngest guy on our stage crew, but he's been around for a while now. I brought Zeke to the P & T crew. Zeke had been adopted when he was in high school by a distant relative of his who is a friend of mine. Zeke was living with this relative in Branson and not doing well there as a punk atheist. No one does well in Branson, it's a shit hole. When his guardian would come visit me in Vegas, I'd talk atheism with the boy, and finally my friend said, "You're helping turn him into an atheist and making Branson hell for him, so let him move in with you." Zeke had just graduated from high school, so he moved into the Slammer and lived with me. I didn't take care of him at all, just gave him a room and let him eat my food. He played video games and watched TV and my friends thought it was sexy to have a good-looking young boy around the house eating Top Ramen in his underwear (how the Top Ramen got into his underwear, you don't want to know). He finally started working with the Penn & Teller show sweeping floors at the shop, and now he's worked his way up to a serious magic guy. I like Zeke. I recapped AB's story for everyone in the Monkey Room. I lightened it up a little bit, since it was still a bit too intense and honest for me to really deal with.

When I finished, I said, "Okay, AB, have at it," and offered him my dinner, salmon and spinach, which turned out to be pretty much kosher. I figured we must have something that wasn't and pointed him to our sandwich and fruit plate.

It was turkey sandwiches, cheese, and pineapple and banana. AB was disappointed. Yeah, technically it wasn't really kosher, because the turkeys probably hadn't been slaughtered with the "correct" procedure, but it also wasn't obscene. He'd tasted versions of all of this stuff. This wasn't the real forbidden-sin food. If he was going to lose his virginity, he wanted to really get fucked.

"So, we're looking for bacon, right?" I asked.

"Yup."

"So, Jonesy, shall we just call room service? I mean, they have good bacon and eggs. How long will that take?"

The Rio All-Suite Hotel and Casino in Las Vegas, Nevada, has great bacon and eggs, and their room service is swift, but we didn't want to wait around even that long. We wanted to watch virgin AB get fucked by the swine *now*.

The steakhouse at the Rio was open all night, and the steakhouse had it all. We decided we'd take him out. Zeke is a punk and Zeke speaks his mind. "Listen, motherfucker," he told AB, "if I go along, you're going to eat all the fucking shit and I'm going to watch you do it. If we go, and you like pussy out on us or something, I'll kick your fucking ass and shove the bacon down your throat and up your Jew ass. Got it?"

AB agreed, and Penn, Teller, Jonesy, Zeke, our MIT buddy, and AB headed to the All-American Bar and Grille. We were laughing and joking, but it was a heavy event. AB was trembling with nervousness. He said later that a lot of his excitement and nervousness was being out with Penn & Teller, but that didn't enter into it. This was a change in his life. This was some sort of improvised atheist baptism.

Before I tell you the rest of AB's story, I need to tell you about another big atheist baptism I hosted. A few years earlier, Joe Rogan of *Fear Factor* and Doug Stanhope of *The Aristocrats* had told me about their favorite performance artist. It was a whack job who went by the name Extreme Elvis. Extreme Elvis is a fat Elvis impersonator with a very small cock. We all know he has a cashew dick, because he performs naked onstage and will often piss on the audience. He has the Elvis sideburns, and the Elvis hair, and a big fat belly, and a little dick, and he sings wonderfully. Most Elvis impersonators fall down on the voice. Elvis could sing his ass off and Extreme Elvis can sing for real. Extreme Elvis doesn't do many shows, because people don't book a naked needle-dick fat guy who pisses in public, and if they do, the police often enter into the situation and stop the show. He can't really do a full show unless he's playing at a private party, and what kind of asshole is going to pay a fat, badly hung, naked, pissing Elvis impersonator to come into his private home?

PENN JILLETTE

I booked Extreme Elvis for a party at my private home. I set up a huge stage, sound system, and lights in my courtyard and invited about a hundred and fifty people, about 135 percent of whom showed up. I booked friends to play all day as opening acts, and Goudeau was there making Elvis deep-fried peanut butter and banana sandwiches.

The party started at about noon, and Extreme Elvis hit the stage around two o'clock the next morning. His show is wonderful. "Every generation gets the Elvis they deserve," he explained, and he gave us that. It was very intense. People who were afraid of naked fat guys and urine were on the second-story catwalk, and the real boys were down front. Extreme Elvis was funny, challenging, inspired, beautiful, and just amazing. We got so much more than we deserved.

Extreme Elvis and I had planned that after his first set, he would take a break before his second set, right before sunrise. I would turn off all the power at the Slammer—not just all the lights, but all the power. No electricity. I have a rather large lap pool, and we were going to put his band in the pool, acoustic guitars and bongos held by musicians floating on rafts while his backup singers were treading water.

The electric set had been confrontational, the theater of cruelty. He'd scared people and made them uncomfortable, and everyone expected the second set to be heavier, like he was going to shit on everyone or something. It *was* heavier, but in a very different way. We had tiki lamps and candles around the pool. There was moonlight. The guitarist strummed softly from the air mattress floating in the pool and Extreme Elvis, naked, sang "Love Me Tender" as he entered the pool like an apparition. Once the whole band was in the pool, I joined them. Elvis weighs more than me, but with the help of buoyancy, I went under between his legs and got him on my shoulders. By candle and tiki light he sang the most gentle and beautiful songs from on top of my shoulders. Soon most everyone took off their clothes and joined us in the water.

He did "Suspicious Minds" and all my musician friends did the backup singing. The pool was filled with naked people and a big fat Elvis singing on my shoulders. When I write that Elvis went to "Kumbaya," you're thinking I mean that figuratively, but no, we were all singing "Kumbaya" and holding hands naked in the pool in a hot Vegas dawn.

It may be important at this point to remind my dear readers that I've never had a sip of alcohol or any recreational drug in my life. My Slammer parties have included a South American man nailing his cock to a board, tying that board to a rope, and using that rope to pull a wagon containing a topless woman across my band room floor (which is carpeted, and I swear, I told him it was carpeted and that this would create more friction before he got there; it was a language problem, not a lack of compassion and foresight on my part). We also had nude cornstarch wrestling, where I wrestled my little-person (they prefer that to "dwarf"; I don't get it, but I don't get African-Americans preferring that to "black," and it's not my decision) Mexican buddy Arturo. His arms weren't long enough to hold his head out of the cornstarch, so our wrestling turned into me saving his life—well, saving his life after being the one to almost drown him in gunk. After my children were born, the Slammer parties featured Nemo, Mickey and Minnie Mouse, and Cinderella instead of cock nailing, nude cornstarch wrestling, and Extreme Elvis, but the same amount of alcohol and recreational drugs was present and that amount is always none.

Holding hands and singing "Kumbaya" with fat, naked, badly hung Extreme Elvis sitting on my shoulders meant a lot to a lot of people. Several people have since told me that when they took off all their clothes and walked into that pool as the sun came up in Vegas and sang "Suspicious Minds," they understood what atheism really was. It was an atheist baptism. Everyone seemed to be changed by it. As I type it, I'm aware that it seems like a crazy person is writing this, but with all the naked-fat-guy-pissing psycho energy of the night, it was mostly just a celebration of living a free and loving life. I guess you had to be there.

As the sun came up, I sat in the hot tub with Extreme Elvis and the very well-hung and hairy porn star Ron Jeremy. Ron Jeremy said it was the best party he'd ever been to, and Ron's been to some parties. I have a picture of me naked, with Extreme Elvis on one side and Ron Jeremy on the other. It could be used in a Trojan condom ad, with the caption "We Fit All Men."

Now back to AB's slightly different atheist baptism. This one was also improvised. We took him into the All-American Bar and Grille and he sat down in the Christ position for the Last Supper. This was his first supper, his atheist communion.

AB didn't order. Teller and I ordered for him. We don't know much about kosher, but we faked it pretty well:

Shrimp cocktail
Crab legs
Clam chowder
Oysters
Pork loin
Barbecue ribs

and a

Bacon cheeseburger, medium rare, with extra cheese and extra *extra* bacon.

Many people have pointed out since that there was no way for us to know that AB didn't have a shellfish allergy. We might have had to deal with anaphylactic shock at our communion. Instead of a born-again atheist, we might have had a dead Jew, and I might be writing this book from the High Desert State Prison, but if your grandmother had had tubes, she might have been a Jewish radio.

The server asked us who was eating what, and we pointed to AB and said he was eating it all, we would just pick.

The pork and bacon cheeseburger took a while, but the chowder and shellfish were out right away. There was a moment when AB just sat there and looked at the food. It was going to be an important moment and he wanted to take a minute and really decide what he was going to do. Teller grabbed the back of AB's head, grabbed a shrimp, and just stuck it in AB's mouth. What's the use of being an atheist if you still have to stand on ceremony? AB chewed the shrimp and kind of shook his head. It was a big moment.

I don't know who died and made Jonesy a Talmudic scholar, but Jonesy said that eating the shrimp really didn't count, that it wasn't the moment, because AB hadn't chosen to eat the *traif*—he had been forced by Teller. Jonesy knows how things look in the eyes of Yahweh. We all agreed that Jonesy was right, and AB considered for a moment, then opened up a crab leg and ate it. That was his defiance of god. If the religious can be silly enough to think that eating the right food makes you religious, we can play along for a meal and pretend that eating the wrong food will make you rational.

He ate the crab leg, and our table erupted into cheers. We sounded like we belonged in a Vegas sports bar. AB wasn't satisfied with the shellfish. He said none of this was really a new taste. There are kosher knockoffs of shellfish. He'd had Krab and fake shrimp. He'd had chowders that had the vibe of clam without the presence of an actual bivalve. It wasn't dirty-filthy-anal-sex-with-two-nuns-on-Easter-Sunday sin.

Teller, Zeke, Jonesy, our MIT friend, and I dug into the shrimp, crab, and chowder. It wasn't an antireligious thing for us; we're entertainers, and when there's food around, we eat.

The pork loin and ribs came and that was no big deal either. He'd had bovine versions. We were all just waiting for the atheist communion wafer, the pure symbol of free thought: the bacon cheeseburger. The All-American Bar and Grille at the Rio makes a fine one. They didn't know how important this one was, but it was the last thing they brought. It was made with loving care.

There it was, on a plate with some fries. A big fat ground-beef patty, medium-rare and juicy, just dripping goodness, with a few slices of cheddar melted on it, and strips, a lot of strips, of bacon, the candy of meat, draped over the top.

You could hear the inspirational music swell. It was the monolith in *2001*, the unholy grail, the covenant to *not* talk to god. We had symbolism up the ass. On that plate with the bacon cheeseburger were Mark Twain, George Carlin, Einstein, Ingersoll, and Butterfly McQueen. Frank Zappa, Martin Mull, Randy Newman, Richard Feynman, Christopher Hitchens, and Richard Dawkins. It was dripping like a hot shiksa. It was the Clash screaming, "You must not act the way you were brought up." It was absolutely free—or at least Teller and I could put it on our hotel tab.

AB looked at all of us. Made eye contact with each of us. Zeke said lovingly, "Do it, motherfucker." AB grinned and picked up the burger. He held it in front of his face with the juice dripping and took a deep whiff. He sucked that good bacon freedom into his lungs and then took a bite.

His eyes widened.

"Goddamn, that's good! Wow!" You can see why those whack jobs keep control over food. It's powerful. It's life. AB was transformed. The next day he would go to a fancy barbershop and get a real shave with a real straight razor. I didn't know it, but that's another thing some Jews can't do: they can't have a razor touch the skin of their face. AB's life changed; it started way before the cheeseburger and it will continue, but I was so proud to be with him for that first bite. It was a celebration. It was one nation under a motherfucking groove.

AB couldn't get over how good bacon was. I tried to imagine tasting bacon for the first time. I can remember my mom putting bacon on the plate with my pancakes. You wouldn't really put the pure Massachusetts (fuck Vermont) maple syrup directly on the bacon, but hey, if a little happened to flow over from the pancakes to the bacon, there was nothing you could do about it, right? I remembered the smell of our kitchen as a child and my mom draining the bacon on a double layer of paper towels. It's a beautiful thing.

AB and I became friends. I'm invited to his divorce party. His children have played with my children. He made sure it was not a high Jewish holiday and his sons wore baseball caps, the headgear of choice for the waffling Jew. Every time AB visits me, he brings me a big package of fancy bacon and some nice artisanal cheeses. He's a good man.

• • •

Last time I was in New York City, I got in a day before I had to work. AB invited me to go to Traif. It's a restaurant in Williamsburg, Brooklyn, on the edge of the Hasidic community. It's the perfect restaurant for AB to take me to. The menu is really good food, and it's mostly *traif.* It's bacon-wrapped dates stuffed with blue cheese. It's pulled-pork sandwiches and bacon doughnuts. The food is great and the food is sacrilegious. My buddy SweetiePie, with the facial hair of the leather daddy in the Village People and from Michigan, was my date. SweetiePie got his nickname when he was our theater manager in Hollywood way back before Off-Broadway. His name was Michael and I asked him if he preferred "Mike" or "Michael." He said "Anything is fine," and I said, "In that case, I shall call you SweetiePie," and it stuck. I think he has a different story about how he got his name, but neither of us is lying. SweetiePie is from as non-Jewish a background as Goudeau and me.

It seemed like such a nutty event that I tweeted it, and because of that, some ex-Hasid Jews showed up. So it was AB, SweetiePie, an African-American model skeptic computer programmer whom AB had brought, a Russian woman who looked like she'd been downloaded from a porn site, a woman documentary filmmaker who was doing a movie on ex-Hasids, and three ex-Hasids. All of the ex-Hasids were men. There certainly are women who no longer believe, but it's even harder for them to get out. They can't fucking drive, for Christ's sake, and maybe "for Christ's sake" is the wrong ejaculation to use there.

So, there we were, nine of us, all brought together to celebrate the flouting of religious dietary laws and have some bacon doughnuts.

The three ex-Hasidic men were in three different stages of breaking away. The one nearest to me was just a guy, a little rockabilly and out of fashion, but still just a guy. He had sideburns, not quite as bushy or big as Extreme Elvis's, but sideburns, very gentile facial hair. He had no hat and hair like an early Jerry Lee Lewis. He moved like and had the aggression of Lenny Bruce, and his face was not dissimilar to Lenny's in his prime. He wore jeans and a shirt. He was in his twenties but talked like Jackie Mason. The sentence structure, accent, and inflections were not American, but he had been born in Brooklyn. He was as American as me, but seemed like a foreigner who'd watched a lot of *Happy Days* episodes to learn how to act. I will call him Sauly. Like a much more Jewish Pauly Shore. Sauly was loud, clumsy, and very lovable.

I'm moving up in level of Jewishness: the second man I will call Moishe. He was a big man, not my size but close. He was wearing a hat that could have been Justin Timberlake's but could also have been Hasidic; you'd have to see the rest of the outfit. But the rest of his outfit wouldn't have told you enough. It wasn't all black, like he was supposed to wear, but wasn't a Hawaiian shirt either. He had *payot,* the Jewish sideburn curls, but they were getting shorter. He had come to Vegas a few months earlier and told me he was really ready to leave Judaism. He wanted me to cut his long curly sideburns, the way I had fed AB a bacon cheeseburger. The hair growing in his sideburn region had been down to his stomach, but lately he had been trimming it back as he felt less Jewish. He still wanted me to do the final cutting, but he was already back to being able to hide his *payot* behind his ears. Moishe was still deeper in the Hasidic world than Sauly. Moishe talked like Jackie Mason if Jackie had never wanted to be on TV. He was obviously from another country. He'd also been born in Brooklyn.

The third ex-Hasid was hard-core. He was full-on guy-working-in-an-NYC-electronics-store. He was a small man, all dressed in black, with a hat, long *payot,* and a beard. He spoke English very well, but with a heavy accent, such an accent that the phrase "such an accent" would start at a middle C and rise up to about a B-flat by the last word. He looked and sounded like a cartoon of a New York Jewish immigrant. His name had no American equivalent. It wasn't a name; it was a word. You know how gentile "Penn Fraser Jillette" sounds? Well, imagine the Jewish form of that. Not really a name, just sounds designed to be ethnic. I'll call him Schmoozleschnu. Schmoozleschnu had been born in Brooklyn, NYC, USA, in 1985. He didn't learn English until 2006, and it was his third language. He was raised speaking Yiddish, and he added

Hebrew probably because it was a little less Jewish. His family didn't have a TV, listen to the radio, or see any movies. He was from another world, and he was a twenty-minute cab ride from the MTV corporate offices in Times Square.

The first nonreligious book he read—not the first book in English, but the first nonreligious book he ever read—was *The God Delusion* by Richard Dawkins. He had his mind blown by the bacon cheeseburger of comedy, George Carlin, when Schmoozleschnu first watched TV.

Mr. Pie and I were about to learn a lot of stuff we never knew and would have a lot of trouble believing.

I guess some of this is common knowledge, or it should be. You know the Pennsylvania Dutch talk nutty, right? We know that there is an enormous Latino population that speaks Spanish and has some different customs than mall Americans. The Amish and the Gypsies have their own style and language, kinda sorta. If you've ever been to Dorchester, Boston, or seen *Gone Baby Gone* or *The Departed,* or been in the Deep South, you know there are still some wild accents in our homogenized country. If you've heard me when I'm not on TV and I'm thinking about my mom and dad, I talk a bit like a Pepperidge Farm salesman. We all know about the diverse cultures of the United States of America. I mean, Christ on Italian beef, have you ever talked to someone from the real Chicago? It'll put you off your feed.

I knew all that, but I didn't know there were people born in the USA who didn't speak any English. We're a nation of immigrants, and immigrants want to assimilate, but not the Hasids. It's a very successful cult. It's a subculture that has nothing to do with the rest of American culture. While they were full-blown Hasids, these guys had never heard of Madonna or the Beatles. They had never heard of Elvis. *They had never heard of Elvis.* They had never fucking heard of Elvis Aaron Presley, the good old boy with the Jewish mother. Moishe used the term "Looney Tunes" to describe the people he used to live with. I asked him how he knew about Looney Tunes. He said he knew them from retailing children's underwear with those cartoons on them. His father had also shown him some Mickey Mouse cartoons on a sixteen-millimeter projector on the wall of their home, and now his father felt that was why Moishe was going crazy and leaving the fold.

Pie and I sat chowing down on bacon-wrapped shellfish while we found out that religious authority figures fucking little boys is not just a Catholic thing. Our new friends all had firsthand experiences. They all had been married to strangers while in their teens. Even in this tightly knit community, the people they were marrying were often strangers. Strangers they would fuck to produce a lot of children. The fucking-through-a-hole-in-the-sheet thing is a myth, but they really do fuck only at night in the dark, and there is no pussy-eating. You can't get crazier than not allowing pussy-eating. Husbands can't even look at their wives' cunts, and this is a community without television. They are more lenient about blow jobs—some sages allow it, some don't—but no matter what they do sexually, marrying a stranger in the twenty-first century is a little weird.

Somehow in the mishmash of finally allowing American culture to flood over them, they had stumbled on me and my radio show's podcasts. There are only a few dozen of these ex-Hasids and they all know each other, so if one of them finds something it moves through the expats pretty fast. Somehow by the weird random path of life, I was in the middle of this group of heroes.

I asked Schmoozleschnu how he was led down the road to atheism. How did he end up eating *traif* at Traif with me? It's the same one-word answer that you get to so many varied questions: pussy. He didn't know anything about science, but he knew about strip clubs. He would go to strip clubs but had never heard of Madonna. It just doesn't seem right. He said that most of the Hasids go to strip clubs and hookers. It seems like at strip clubs, American culture would wash over you, but I guess if you're in a hat and funny clothes you still stay separate enough for god. Schmoozleschnu was getting a lap dance from a dancer and he asked her what religion she was. He asked her that because . . . well, I don't know, I guess because he was a crazy motherfucker. She said, "Atheist." Why don't I ever get "dancers" like that? It seems all the dancers I see have big old hateful crosses hanging between their big brand-spankin'-new lovable tits, but Schmoozleschnu got lucky. "Getting lucky" in this case doesn't mean getting laid, but rather having your entire philosophic underpinnings destroyed. He had never believed it really possible to be an atheist. All he had heard about us, in Yiddish I suppose, was that we were miserable monsters. And here was a miserable monster getting his circumcised dick hard. When I have a hard-on I want to talk evolution, and so did Schmoozleschnu. He asked her if she believed in evolution, and of course she did. He said he would disprove it, while she was rubbing her perfectly evolved ass over the burlap, or whatever, of his black trousers.

Schmoozleschnu thought he had a killer argument: which was more complicated, a tomato or a pair of eyeglasses? A tomato, of course. And yet we believe that eyeglasses are designed and a tomato is not? (Read that sentence making your voice go way up, like a high school student in the 1950s playing Shylock.) Our busty dancing Charles Darwin pointed out that a tomato and eyeglasses were different and then laid on the origin of the species for Schmoozleschnu in a loud club. Maybe she used some visual aids and pulled aside her G-string as she explained how we got from primordial ooze to poontang in a billion years. She covered geology and disputed the young earth and Noah's ark, and he left with a happy ending and a better understanding about how happy endings had come into existence.

Pussy in a strip club led Schmoozleschnu to the big D's and H's—Dawkins, Dennett, Hitchens, and Harris—and then to supper with me and SweetiePie in Brooklyn. Sauly was totally American; Moishe was on his way but still able to pass for religious around his family; and Schmoozleschnu was still looking full Yama Yama Jew. I like to think that the term "Yama Yama Jew" is poetic enough that I don't have to explain, but I will. I went to Ringling Brothers & Barnum and Bailey the Greatest Show on Earth Clown College in Florida. I was the last picked and the youngest the year I went. I took classes in trapeze, wire walking, and prop building. It was a very extensive program, six days a week, and on the seventh day I had remedial makeup. I wasn't good. I learned to do a double backflip on the trampoline and to walk across a tight-wire. I learned that I really, really sucked at physical comedy. I came into college as a great juggler, and I left as a great juggler, but I never got to be even a passable clown. That's right, I failed as a fucking clown.

We were taught in makeup class, and in *makeup* makeup class, that you should never put any red or black makeup on your upper lip—the whole exaggerated mouth is painted on the lower lip and chin. If you put any mouthlike makeup above your mouth, it obscures your facial expressions instead of magnifying them, and when you open your mouth it's just a slightly bigger hole in the middle of a red blotch. If the makeup is only painted below the upper lip, then all your expressions are exaggerated, and on people other than me it's funny. Clown makeup that's put on both the upper and lower lip gives a look that professional clowns call a "busted asshole." Once you've heard the term "busted asshole" for that kind of mouth makeup, well, it'll add some *Human Centipede* images to your nightmare idea of bad clowns.

The other big indicator of a sucky clown is a Yama Yama suit. A real clown has a costume that in some way signals a specific character. The clothes also have to give the performer the ability to move, tumble, juggle, run, and fall down. The costume should amplify body movement like the makeup amplifies facial expressions. Yama Yama suits are those one-piece zip-up-the-front baggy suits with bright colors, like Zippy the Pinhead wears. Yama Yama suits obscure body movement like a busted asshole obscures facial expressions. Now that you know, you'll spot lots of Yama Yama suits and busted assholes on bad clowns.

I was once talking to another clown college alumnus about getting a good deal on a video recorder at Forty-seventh Street Photo in New York City. He said, "Is that the place with the Yama Yama Jews?" It's the perfect term.

Schmoozleschnu was full Yama Yama because that was his job. Because his English was so good, and because he could work on Friday nights and all day Saturday, he was in showbiz. He was a professional Yama Yama Jew. If you're watching an NYC show that has a Hasidic Jew in the background, that extra is probably my new friend Schmoozleschnu. He's also a TV and movie consultant on all kinds of wacky Jewish sects. He makes sure they get it right, and they can talk to him in English and on Saturdays.

The last time I asked anyone if they were Jewish was many years ago at MIT. I don't remember why, but I asked a genius geek who was showing us around the Media Lab, the same genius geek who joined us for AB's atheist communion, if he was Jewish. He responded, "No, I'm an atheist." His dad, as a young child, had fought and escaped from the Nazis, but that didn't make his family Jewish. He didn't see it as a racial or cultural question but a theological question. He didn't care what Hitler would have considered him; he was an atheist. He was no more a Jew than I was a Christian. That answer was important to me. It was that moment when I understood George Clinton suggesting one nation under a motherfucking groove. It was an inspiration.

I don't understand atheists who claim to also be Jewish. I've wanted to do a *Bullshit!* episode on cultural Jews and tribalism, but there's no way Showtime would consider letting us do that. They're afraid that cultural Jews would be better at letter-writing than friends of Motherfucking Teresa, and they're probably right about that. I hear hard-core atheists claim that they are Jewish because their moms were Jewish. That's not a genetic rule, that's a religious rule, and if you're not religious, you don't follow religious rules. There were rules in the South for what makes someone "colored," how many drops of Negro blood it took. There is no scientific taxonomy for different races; there are no genetic markers. It's very hard for me to tell what religion my mother-in-law is; I guess she'd call herself spiritual. I believe my wife's grandmother, whom I adore, might call herself atheist. My wife was certainly raised atheist, and yet there are some people who would think our children should be considered Jewish because someone in the maternal lineage said that. Nope. They are atheist and their culture is Vegas—and even that's too much tribalism for me. Family matters. I love my mom and dad, and my sister and nephews and children. I identify with them. But I don't see how being identified with people you've never met because of "race" is anything but racism, pure and simple. Being proud of yourself, your beliefs, your taste, your accomplishments, and your immediate family and friends seems sensible and right. Being proud of some imaginary group you were born into seems insane and wrong. It's collectivism at its worst, and collectivism at its worst is racism. I went back to Newfoundland to see where my grandfather grew up, but I'm not a Newfoundland-American, I'm Penn Jillette, son of Sam and Valda, husband of Emily, father of Moxie and Zolten. Penn Jillette, an asshole who didn't even do well in Ringling Brothers and Barnum & Bailey the Greatest Show on Earth Clown College.

I do think cultures should be studied and preserved. I think it's important that the great ideas of the Jewish people are preserved, but I don't see why they have to be preserved by people who consider themselves Jews. Spike Lee could do *Schindler's List* and Clint Eastwood can do *Bird*. I don't think that complexion or lineage should determine what groups you belong to. I have more in common with Richard Feynman, George Clinton, Sun Ra, and Tiny Tim than I do white Christians. I am an atheist whack job; that's my culture.

Schmoozleschnu was a professional Jewish expert, and his not considering himself Jewish is a big step toward utopia, world peace, and one nation under a motherfucking groove.

At Traif that night, Pie and I heard amazing stories about life as a Hasid. All the men would ritually bathe naked together every morning. They were all taught it's okay to steal from a gentile. They had an education that covered the minutiae of prayer and very little mathematics or history. Our new friends were sure part of an insane cult, but none of them had left it completely yet, and I don't blame them. The ideas of the Hasids are scientifically and morally wrong; the fashion, food, and lifestyle are way stupid; but the community and family make me envious.

When I lived in Greenfield, Massachusetts, with my mom and dad, with my sister and her family a couple miles away, I was in a town where most everyone had known me since my birth. I was around people every day who knew me and cared for me—and didn't agree with me on anything. I watched Tiny Tim and Lawrence Welk on TV with my mom and dad. Dad hated Tiny, I hated Lawrence, and we loved each other.

Now I live in Las Vegas. We have a big fence and gates around our house. I don't know the name of anyone who lives on our street. My children have four aunts who are still alive and have never seen all of them in one room at one time. They have a grandfather, and a step-grandmother, and a grandmother, all of whom they love and are loved by, and they see them a few times a year, and never all together. They have a great-grandmother, who is great, and they see her a couple times a year. Day to day, my children are part of a very small family. Technology like Skype allows them to talk to their extended family, but as wonderful as that is, it's not living near them.

My wife and I disagree about art and poker, but other than that, I'm rarely in a room with someone who loves me and disagrees with me. It's something I miss in my life. Technology has given us a wonderful world, but it has also spread us out. We have babysitters instead of aunts. Dying more than thirty miles from where you were born is a pretty new thing in human history. There are some emotional family bumps on this road to the future.

The Hasidic Jews have problems, lots of problems, lots of weird crazy shit to fuck people up and make them waste their lives, but they do have family and community in spades.

I know how much I miss my mom, dad, and sister. I know how much I missed them when they were alive and I talked to them every day on the phone—I was still thousands of miles away.

I can't imagine how difficult it is for these ex-Jews. They are working to love science, and to love the truth, and to be honest, but it's costing them dearly. Their marriages were arranged, but they still have a great deal of affection for their wives. They love their children. They love their siblings, and they have plenty of them—that's the way the Hasids keep a growing population. They don't have a lot of people converting to their fucking psychosis. They love their moms and dads and uncles and aunts and the entire safe community that they're giving up.

They are giving all that up for the truth. They are heroes, they are astronauts. And I was sitting with them and they were talking about my radio show as we ate food together. Food that everyone they loved for their whole lives thought was evil food.

Schmoozleschnu said that after the stripper taught him science and he read Dawkins and listened to George Carlin and then my radio show (why the fuck am I in that list?), he knew there was no god. He had the moment when there was no doubt in his mind that there was no god. There's another way to say that: he had reached the moment when there was nothing but doubt in his mind. The moment when he couldn't accept nonsense on faith.

When he had lost his faith and seen the light of reason peeking through, he asked himself one question: "Who will take care of me?"

Pie and I almost cried when he said that. I haven't believed in god for so long that I don't remember ever feeling that god was watching out for me. My family watched out for me. My mom and dad took care of me, and now my wife and friends take care of me. I look in my son's four-year-old eyes, and I don't feel alone. He knows something in his heart that can keep me going. But Schmoozleschnu lost god, and all his family and friends were staying behind with his imaginary friend. A silly dream goes away and takes with it your whole real life. He can listen to my radio show, and he can have supper with me, but I'm not going to take care of him. I have my own family and friends.

The restaurant check came and I threw down my AmEx and they didn't take AmEx, so I went for my Visa card. Moishe and Schmoozleschnu, with their hats and *payot,* grabbed the check away from me: "No, no, we've got it." Sauly pointed out it was the only time anyone would ever see two Hasids fighting with a goy to pay the check. That's sure what it looked like, but there were no Hasids or goyim at that table; that table was becoming one nation under a motherfucking groove.

We said good-bye, and Moishe drove Pie, the filmmaker, and me back to midtown Manhattan. He drove us through the Hasid community where he'd lived his whole life. The community he loved and was trying to leave. He said that if I walked down these streets in the daytime I would be considered as foreign as if I were in a town two hundred clicks out of Beijing. Moishe put a Hasidic singer on the car CD player, and even the scale and the mode of the pop music was foreign to us. Moishe translated that the singer was singing about the joy of the end of the world. Whiskey Tango Foxtrot?

Moishe had talked to his father about becoming an atheist. Moishe felt his dad loved him but was still secretly hoping Moishe would end up in jail or something, some deep trouble, to vindicate the faith of his father. Moishe said his dad had asked him if he was happier without religion. If he was happier without his family and community. If he was happier as an atheist.

Moishe had explained to his father that what made him happy didn't matter; what mattered was the truth.

That may be the definition of a hero.

"One Nation Under a Groove"

—George Clinton

Postscript: Since our dinner, Schmoozleschnu has come completely out of the closet. He is doing a lot of consulting work and even writing scripts about the Hasids. He's now proud of his journey and would like me to give his real name, Luzer Twersky—yup, it's pronounced "loser." Maybe we all need to take care of him.

The Bible's Second Commandment

Thou shalt not make for thyself an idol, whether in the form of anything that is in heaven above, or that is on the earth beneath, or that is in the water under the earth; for I the Lord thy God am a jealous God, visiting the iniquity of the fathers upon the children to the third and the fourth generation of those who hate Me, but showing steadfast love to thousands of those who love Me and keep My Commandments.

Maybe the most important part of my philosophy is that most people are good. If you run into a Starbucks and throw your car keys to the first person you see and say, "My wife is having a baby, I have to jump into her car and drive her to the hospital. My Porsche [I wish I knew cars, so I could give a good example of a fancy car, but I drive a Mini Cooper] is double-parked—could you take it, move it, and . . . here's my cell phone, just call "Mommy" on there and tell us where it's parked . . ." If you say that to most people (providing you pick them and they don't pick you) they're going to do the right thing. Your car and cell phone are going to be safe whether you throw those keys to an atheist, Muslim, Jew, Christian, or Jain.

ONE ATHEIST'S SECOND SUGGESTION

Do not put things or even ideas above other human beings. (Let's scream at each other about Kindle versus iPad, solar versus nuclear, Republican versus Libertarian, Garth Brooks versus Sun Ra—but when your house is on fire, I'll be there to help.)

Pastor Shirley, My Mom and Dad, Lesbians, and Jesus Christ

I think it was Thomas Jefferson who said, "And were it left to me to decide whether we should have a Christianity without lesbians or lesbians without a Christianity, I should not hesitate a moment to prefer the latter . . ." My parents certainly felt that way.

My mom was in her mid-eighties when she first declared herself an atheist. She dragged my sister with her into the denial of god. My dad and brother-in-law still called themselves Christians and believed in god until their deaths, but they quit the church along with their wives.

I became an atheist when I was in high school. Our family was very active in the First Congregational Church of Greenfield, Massachusetts, the First Church of the Covered-Dish Supper. My dad led the choir; my mom organized some of the ham suppers and maple sugar eats. She helped with coffee hour after the service and used the leftover coffee to make one of the haggises of New England food, coffee "Jell-O." These nutty Christian ladies would take an urn of leftover black coffee; put in some Knox gelatin, no sugar, no nothing; pour it into big cake pans; and put it in the fridge to gel up. The next night it was cut into squares and served with dairy topping at some Monday-night potluck as a weird black bitter speed-freak dessert. My sister sang in the choir and did all the bookkeeping for the church, and my brother-in-law was part of the grounds committee and helped keep the building in good repair. The First Congo (as people in Greenfield called it) had been around since 1754, and when my family finally quit the church, we had that whole time covered. We had over a quarter of a millennium in combined believer-pack years at that church.

For my part, I was baptized there, and one of my first jobs before my dishwashing career was mowing the church lawn and trimming the church bushes (I mean that literally; we haven't gotten to lesbianism yet). I went to church every Sunday until high school, when I negotiated a deal where I could sleep in on Sundays, after my Saturday late-night rock and roll monkeying, providing I went to youth group on Sunday evening. We had a liberal pastor when I was growing up, and he encouraged discussions. I decided to read the Bible.

Reading the Bible is the fast track to atheism. Reading the Bible means starting at "In the beginning . . ." and throwing it down with disgust at ". . . the grace of the lord Jesus be with all. Amen." I'm sure there are lots of religious people who've read the Bible from start to finish and kept their faith, but in my self-selected sample, all the people I know who have done that are atheists.

After reading the Bible, I started arguing with the pastor. At first he encouraged me to ask anything. I started listening to Martin Mull, Randy Newman, and Frank Zappa for my atheist music. I read "Why I Am Not a Christian" and *Catch-22,* and lots of Vonnegut. My discussions with the pastor got better and better, and then they got really great, and then . . . he needed to have a little talk with my parents. He explained to them that I wasn't getting much out of youth group. He told them, with a laugh, that I was converting the other children to atheism. He told my mom and dad that I should just read and think on my own. He shut me the fuck up, and I was thrilled about it. My quitting the church was sanctioned by the church. Sweet! My mom and dad couldn't very well argue with the minister about my religious education, so I got a free walk out of church. I was the first in the family to split.

My dad was not a Bible thumper, but he had a deep belief. When he died, we respected his wishes and had a minister at the graveside services. It was just our family, and my mom took the minister aside to say, "We're all atheists. Sam wanted to have you here, but keep it short; none of us believe." I don't know if my mom lost her faith or if she never really believed. She liked church music and hearing her husband sing in the choir. She liked seeing her young son with his hair combed once a week. I like to give credit to writers, artists, and myself for my atheism, but, like everything else, it's probably all my mom. I remember her saying to me after church, "I believe that when you die, that's it." That may not be out-and-out atheism, but you can sure see the entrance ramp from there.

My dad was still praying for me the week he died. He was so proud of me and loved me so much and supported me in everything I did. He tried to assert that I was a good Christian because I lived my life in a way he mostly approved of. I tried to tell him that denying Jesus Christ as lord really did make "good Christian" hard to stick, but he kept saying, "When I get to heaven, I'm going to have to do a lot of talking to persuade them to let my wife and children in, but I'll do it." He lived through the Depression and, with only my mom helping, built the house we lived in. They carried every cinder block and hammered every nail, by themselves. If there is a heaven, with him up there to lobby for me I'm a shoo-in.

My mom and dad were elderly when Pastor Shirley was hired as minister at the First Congo. My mom was thrilled to have a woman in charge, and my dad liked Pastor Shirley. She lived with her female friend, and when Pastor Shirley would come and visit, my dad would ask when she was going to find herself a husband. He wasn't making a joke, he was making conversation. It never crossed his mind that Shirley's roommate might be more than a friend. Pastor Shirley was kind to my mom and dad. At this point in their lives, they couldn't get to church without a lot of help, but she came calling and would do what all visitors were forced to do: talk about me and sometimes watch a video of Penn & Teller's latest Letterman or *SNL*.

This book is not your best choice for information on the politics of the United Church of Christ, but as I remember, the whole organization was taking a vote about the "Open and Affirming" policy around 1985. Some ministers brought it to their congregations to vote on whether the United Church of Christ should accept gays, but Pastor Shirley didn't. As I understood it, she just said "Fuck yeah!" (or whatever church talk for that is) and sent in First Congo's okay. The church elders, who in this church were really way elder, went flip city. The way my mom explained it, these "old men" were very frightened by lesbians. They figured that Northampton was only a half hour away, and Northampton, with Smith College, is seen as the Frisco of Sappho. Were they really afraid of a flood of lesbians driving north on I-91 to get a taste of that small-town "open and affirming" pussy eating? That's not the way my mom put it, but it sure was how I understood it.

The end began when my sister went to all the trouble to get wheelchairs and help my mom and dad into the car and get them to church. When they got there, instead of coffee Jell-O and Cool Whip, they got a bunch of old men trash-talking hot girl-on-girl minister action. They were scheming to force Pastor Shirley out of her job. Maybe the ostensible reason was that she hadn't brought the vote to the church, or maybe they were honest enough to say outright that it was her sexuality, but my mom and dad were having none of it. They took the old New England libertarian position that it was none of anyone's business. One of the anti-diesel-pastor folks said, "Read your Bible," and pointed out a passage or two that said god wasn't thrilled with same-sex sex. My mom responded, "Phooey on your Bible!"

She meant it. My mom didn't use obscenities. Her two strongest ejaculations were "GD" and "phooey." I think she might have said "shit" in my presence once, but it was after most of her body was paralyzed—you gotta give an old girl a break at that point. I never heard her use the word "fuck" or "cocksucker"; "cunt" and "felching" were never mentioned. "Phooey" was strong language for a proper New England woman in her eighties. I never used obscenities around my mom and dad.

They died before my movie *The Aristocrats,* about the dirtiest joke ever, and our obscenely named and themed show *Penn & Teller: Bullshit!* came out. I always wonder if I would have done any of those if Mom and Dad had still been alive. Probably not. It would have embarrassed them too much to be worth it. My mom read my interviews in *Rolling Stone* and *Playboy* and said, "It's amazing how they have to add all that swearing to how you talk to make it fit in their magazine." I didn't want to leave that lie hanging. I explained that I really did talk like that, I just tried to be respectful around her. She shrugged. I'm not sure she really believed me. I've always sworn a fuck of a lot, but I never swore in front of Mom and Dad.

"Phooey on your Bible!" was the end of my mom in that church, and in theism. My dad was still a believer, but he was disgusted with the First Congo. He didn't have any idea that Pastor Shirley was a lesbian, and really neither did anyone else. I had met her and I made some jokes to my parents about her not being much more of a lesbian than Gertrude Stein, but my dad didn't like that. He didn't know or care if I was right, he just knew it was none of my business. It was none of my business and it was none of his business and it was none of the elders' business. Their nosiness made him sick. They were forcing Pastor Shirley out of her job for something that was none of their business. Crimes against nature didn't bug my dad, but he had a zero-tolerance policy for crimes against privacy. Pastor Shirley did her job as minister, and she was kind to him, and what she did with her friend in their house was her own business. He kept a faith in god in his heart and prepared arguments to get Mom, my sister, and me into heaven, but when they got rid of Pastor Shirley, he was out of the church. My mom and dad always gave generously to the church, and they had already made their pledges through the end of that year. Even with Pastor Shirley gone, they didn't go back on that promise. They left the church but still sent in their tithe until the end of the year.

My sister and brother-in-law did the same. The next time she saw me, my sister said to me, "You were right. You've been preaching your atheism to us for thirty years, and you're just right. These are church people acting like this. That's wrong. There's so much suffering and unkindness in the world. There's no god."

My sister gave notice to the church that they needed to phase in another bookkeeper, and my brother-in-law resigned from all his grounds committees. My sister made plans to take all the money that they had budgeted for the church in future years and use it for good causes. They started with bulletproof vests for local police and "jaws of life" for ambulances. Hey, you talk against lesbians around my fucking family, we take you down to Chinatown.

I was doing the Penn & Teller show in New York City when all this happened. I had met Pastor Shirley, and she was very respectful of my atheism. She sincerely cared for my parents, and her view of religion seemed to center on kindness. I liked her. I spoke with her honestly about our disagreements and my gratitude for the solace she brought my parents. When my mom called to tell me the story and explain how they all had quit the church, I was flabbergasted. I cried on the phone. I was so proud of them.

I have a good friend from Louisiana. He's a bit older than I. He talked about his dad being raised a racist. It was just the way things were. In the sixties his dad and the whole community changed. Racism was wrong. That generation really did change. Racism didn't vanish overnight—it's still with us today—but it started to go away. My friend threw me a challenge. He asked me, if I was presented with absolute proof that racism was the correct way to think, would I be able to change? Could I make as deep a change in my worldview as his dad had? I don't know.

Is there something that could make me join a church? Maybe my mom was always a heathen. Maybe my dad didn't get rid of his faith, he just left the church. But it still seems like leaving that church was a difficult, heroic act. Whenever I'm confronted with big changes around me, I think about my mom and dad sticking up for Pastor Shirley. They stuck up for her and still kept their financial pledges. Goddamn.

When I stopped crying, I gave my mom some advice. I warned her that she had to be strong. I said, "Pastor Shirley is going to come by the house one of these days, and she'll thank you for your support, but she'll tell you that your faith is more important than the petty politics of one church. She'll say the church is more important than a few individuals. She'll say that you must keep your faith and keep the community of the church. That's the way it works. You're going to have to be strong and stick to your beliefs." Yeah, I was telling my mom and dad how to be strong. That's the kind of asshole I am.

I was right. Pastor Shirley did stop by the house a while later for a visit.

She thanked them for their support, told them she'd found a job in a church far away, and then inquired about their health and asked how I was doing in New York City.

That's all. Not a word about their going back to the church or to religion.

Phooey on my cynicism.

"We Shall Overcome"

—Pete Seeger

"Jesus Is Easy"

—Martin Mull

Auto-Tune, Tattoos, and Big Fake Tits

Penn Jillette's first rule of tits: all that matters about them love jugs is how much the person whom they're attached to likes them. I've heard a lot of men complain about "fake tits." They'll say stuff like "Those aren't real." They don't mean they're just imagining them, they mean these particular ganastahagans are not genetically coded. In my experience, the men who say this are men with very little experience with aftermarket heavers. Women who have had their breasts altered often like their surgically "enhanced" breasts more, and if they like them more, I like them more.

The Eskimos—or as I think they're called, the Inuits, or maybe the correct term is now "Frozen-Ass Aboriginal North Americans," I don't know—do not have twenty-something words for snow. That's not true. But the Brits do have more than a hundred and fifty terms for male masturbation. If you're in England and someone uses a verb and you don't know what it means, it probably means jacking off. For jilling off, female masturbation, our brothers and sisters across the pond stick to "auditioning the finger puppets." In the good old US of A, if you have a plural noun and you don't know what it means, it probably means breasts. I can't think of a plural noun whose meaning I don't know that wouldn't be better off meaning "tits"—jelutongs!

One of the quickest ways for a man to make me uncomfortable is to talk about strip clubs. I'm very judgmental about how men enjoy strip clubs. If I hear a man say anything negative about a stripper's body, I never seem to get over thinking that guy is a little creepy. I've been to strip clubs with fat men who'll call a woman a third their size "chubby." It makes me crazy. I just overflow with hatred. I can't defend my position. It's not logical, it's emotional. It's fine to judge an entertainer even if you can't do what that entertainer does. You are welcome to come to our show, not being able to do a lick of magic, and say we suck. Even if you couldn't be funny riding the ass of a smoking monkey, you're welcome to judge a comedian's ability to tell a joke. We all judge people who are doing things that we can't do, but if you do it in a strip club in front of me, I'll remember that for as long as I know you and I'll hold it against you. I find it really unpleasant. To me, working in the sex industry isn't about what you're showing off, it's that you're showing it off at all. That's what I love about it.

I used to go to strip clubs a lot. One night I walked in and Valentino was sitting with a bunch of dancers at his table. You don't know who Valentino is. You shouldn't know who Valentino is. You don't even care who Valentino is, but I'm going to tell you. Years ago Valentino was on shitty TV as "the Masked Magician." He did a few shitty TV specials where he pretended to give away shitty magic secrets while wearing a shitty mask so no one would know who he really was. It wasn't really a mask, it was more a black and silver bag over his head. He didn't really give away secrets, because no one would watch that. The way you keep real magic secrets is to make them uninteresting. The way you keep magic secret is by making the secrets really ugly.

The secret to one of the greatest magic tricks you've ever seen is public information; it's patented. You could search for it right now. I'm not going to say which trick it is, because I don't want to piss off the magician even more than I already have, but if you think about one of the best tricks, really any of the best tricks, the secrets are out there and you can find them. If you go to the U.S. Patent Office website (while you're there, search for "Penn Jillette"; I have a patent on a female masturbation device called the "JillJet"—really; I care about women cumming) and search for the best trick you ever saw, it's there. It's a cool, cool trick, but the method is ugly. You won't get through two pages before you lose interest. You'll skim over the diagrams. That's what keeps professional magic secrets secret: they're ugly and boring. Genius magic designer Jim Steinmeyer said the real secret of magic is that we magicians are all guarding an empty safe. There are no real secrets in magic. We do things just the way they have to be done. We sneak things around, we use gaffer's tape, and we lie. Whenever they do a TV detective show with a magic trick as part of the plot, the secret has to be a forty-five-degree-angle mirror. In a detective show, there has to be an "a-ha." You don't get "a-ha" in real life. Real-life detectives don't get it, and real-life magicians don't use it. When Penn & Teller give away magic tricks, it's really hard work. We have to design magic that's made to be exposed. We make the way we do it as beautiful as the trick. That's a sneaky thing for us to do. It makes the audience think that the tricks we don't give away are also beautiful, and that fucks up their shit. When you're looking for something beautiful and satisfying, it's much harder to find the ugly truth.

The big secret of magic is we are willing to work harder to accomplish something stupid than you can imagine. We'll practice things for years that you wouldn't consider investing an hour in. You can imagine spending half your life under a bridge learning to play sax like Sonny Rollins, but you can't imagine spending five minutes learning to drop a palmed cell phone into a little pocket behind a cardboard cutout of Criss Angel while hanging a cross around its neck and talking a mile a minute without the slightest pause. I had to practice that a lot. A lot more than you can imagine. I had to practice it a lot more than you think it's worth. Our big secret is that it's worth more to us to do our tricks than you can even imagine. Our deep secret is simply misplaced priorities.

Shitty Valentino and Fox TV had to pretend magicians were mad at them for exposing secrets. It was pretty embarrassing and desperate. I remember a TV crew following Lance Burton and me to dinner, trying to get us to say we were pissed at the Masked Magician. We didn't care. We gave them nothing. They got a few amateur magicians, starving to be on TV, to act pissed off, but professionals didn't care. Valentino was a two-bit dove magician in Laughlin, Nevada, and he became the Masked Magician and thought he was a big star.

At the strip club that night, Valentino was surrounded by women whose job it was to be sitting around whoever sat down with money. He's one of these really creepy guys who goes to a strip club and acts like he's on a date. He was talking to the women instead of having them rub their asses against his cock. That's really creepy. Sex isn't creepy, loneliness is creepy. Valentino thought some of the women recognized me, and he beckoned me over to his hired table full of hired women. "Hey, Penn, I was just telling these beautiful ladies that I was the Masked Magician and they don't believe me." Has any non-dipshit man ever used the word "ladies" not followed by the word "room"? But he wasn't done. "Would you tell these fine ladies that that's me, that I'm the star, I am the Masked Magician?"

I stood in front of Valentino and his "ladies" (even typing that makes my skin crawl) and started listing names: "David Letterman, Deborah Harry, Picasso, Mick Jagger, Madonna, Ke$ha, Bill Clinton, Mark Twain, Tom Jones, Fergie, Salvador Dalí, Muhammad Ali, Elvis Presley, Ayn Rand, Che Guevara, Ringo Starr, Janet Jackson, Frank Sinatra, Bette Midler, Cher . . ." I went on and on, yelling over the music. After about twenty names from politics, science, and the arts, I asked, "What do all these people have in common?"

Valentino and his "ladies" shrugged their shoulders, jiggling their bountiful jelutongs. I gave them time to think, and then I yelled, "We know who they are because they didn't put fucking bags over their heads when they worked." I paused for another moment and then looked all the women in the eyes, ignoring Valentino, as I said, "I have no idea who this asshole is."

Aftermarket tits fill me with joy when they're cartoony and obvious.

I love them when they look like someone stapled some skin over a Tupperware set. I only find them depressing when women get them to "fix" something. There are medical problems that have to really be fixed, of course, but I'm not talking about that kind of "fixed." I'm talking when they're not happy with their tits because they're "too small" or "too saggy." I'm not saying it's wrong to do it, but it's depressing to me when women use surgery to try to be "normal." I like when surgery is used as a celebration of nutty desire. I like surgery when it's a "fuck you" to god. When the tits are sticking out like Hummer headlights on a Big Wheel tricycle. I like them to be a celebration of choice over nature.

I don't have any tattoos. I'm typing this in a Vegas Starbucks, and everyone has a tattoo. Tattoos used to mean you lived outside the law; now tattoos mean you've been to a mall. You now have Miss Americas with tramp stamps. How depressing is that? It's not depressing because it makes Miss Americas more like sluts, it's depressing because it makes sluts more like Miss Americas. I like sluts; I don't like Miss Americas. I'm old enough that tattoos still seem a little carny and prison, but that image is fading even with me.

My friend, mentor, and hero Doc Swan is a carny. He's a real carny. He's my age, but he's from another time. He taught me fire-eating, and he taught me about friendship. He broke my heart once by telling me that I *used to be* the funniest person he'd ever met. He said I used to be like Curly Howard in the real world, but the day I did Letterman for the first time, I stopped being funny just to be funny—I was now only funny for money. I don't think I was ever as funny as Doc thought I was, but it's certain that something was lost in my heart when I walked out on that Letterman soundstage. Some of my young desperation for attention was replaced with control. Doc loves me enough to tell me. He loves me enough to be sad as he watches me on TV in his motor home parked in a Wal-Mart parking lot, illegally using their storm drain for his gray water.

Doc told me a story about a fire-eater that he knew. Doc said that even for a carny, this fire-eater was really far out. There's a carny story that I've had verified by two different liars. There was a carny named

Vinnie the Puke who had scammed a big rig driver. I don't know what they say this Vinnie did, but let's say he took the driver for some serious jingle. The trucker found out that Vinnie the Puke was with the show and followed the show to the next town to beat payback out of him. The trucker parked his eighteen-wheeler, walked onto the lot, grabbed the first person who looked "with it," and demanded to be taken to Vinnie the Puke. The roustabout responded, "Which one?" He wasn't fucking around. This is a profession that can support two Vinnie the Pukes on a single show. (Doc was telling another carny about my writing this section of the book, and when he told the story, the carny stopped him and asked, "Vinnie the Puke or Benny the Puke?") And, even in that world, Doc says this fire-eater was out there.

Doc said this fire-eater creep didn't want to spend money on food at the cookhouse, so he would eat out of the midway trash. He'd just reach in and finish half-eaten hot dogs and cores of candy apples. Of course there's still good eating in carny trash, but it's a little sickening. There are researchers trying to find out if part of the allergy problems in the USA are caused by too much cleanliness. Doc supplied the anecdotal evidence that this fire-eating pig was never sick.

Doc would tell me how this man had no respect whatsoever for his body. He didn't care what he ate and didn't care about his hygiene, and he was meaner than a snake. Doc once saw his ankle and there were some very odd tattoos. Just weird kinds of angles and marks. Doc asked him what the tattoos meant. "Fuck you," the fire-eater explained. Doc caught him another time, after the fire-eater had found some liquor in the trash and was in a better mood, and asked him again. The fire-eater told Doc that the marks on his ankle didn't mean anything. The fire-eater had been paid five bucks to fix someone's tattoo gun. He'd fixed it and had to test it to make sure it worked. He tested it like you'd test a Bic pen on the back of a candy wrapper. He had his legs crossed, so he just scribbled on his ankle to make sure the gun was fixed. They were the only tattoos he had. Tattoos that didn't mean anything.

Those tattoo scribbles mean the world to me. Those scribbles on his ankle are pure atheist symbols. They show that god, the higher power, nature, the order of things, doesn't mean anything. We are only here for a little while, and our bodies belong to ourselves and no one else. There's no need for respect for a creator because there is no creator. I love those ankle scribbles, but I could never have them. Mine would mean something, and by meaning something would mean nothing.

Teller and I did a bit on Conan where Teller carved the name of Conan's "freely selected" card into my arm. I've written a lot about "tattoos of blood." Those are tattoos without ink. All the pain and none of the gain. Tattoo ink is a lubricant and a coagulant, so tattoos of blood hurt more and bleed more than a real tattoo and they last about three years. So, the same length of time as most of my relationships. It's really just carving into your skin. Teller carved the selected card into my arm on Conan. There was no trick to that part, he just carved in my arm on TV. Teller and I had to practice—we had to put more time into learning it than you'd believe it's worth. That's always how we fool you. We had to practice the card force, but we also had to make sure that I could focus and do the magic moves while my skin was being carved. We had bought an unlicensed tattoo gun and it arrived at our shop. I was wearing cutoffs (it's the desert, and with my body, you gotta wear the Daisy Dukes and feature the talent). While I was waiting for Teller and the crew to get the cards and start working the script, I fired up the gun and just scribbled on my leg, making cuts and letting the blood flow. Trying to see my intelligence, vitality, and passion as outside of nature and my body. It wasn't secret cutting. I can't pretend to understand why young people, mostly women, cut themselves up. I won't write about that, except to write that what I was doing was different from that. And it was different from the carny pig, because it was self-conscious. I was writing "fuck you" to god in blood on my leg, and I knew it, so it wasn't as good.

These tattoos that are walking by me in Starbucks as I write this are tribal and Asian, and some outright religious. I figure the Asian logogram that the trendy guy thinks means "truth" probably means "round-eyed sodomite," but what do I know?

But to me, even the overtly religious ink says "fuck you" to god. (Take this with a grain of salt—to me, *Green Acres* reruns on Nick at Nite are a "fuck you" to god.) Tattoos and big fake tits are a way to say to yourself and the world that the way you ended up, even the way you think you were created, is not as important as your free will. God wanted the back of your neck to have a cute little freckle at your hairline, but you think "Property of Wolf" is more to your liking. God wanted a mole right on your miniskirt line, and you'd rather have "Heaven's Above" and a little pinstripe.

If there really were a god, wouldn't he have the power and wisdom to put that Playboy bunny on your ass at birth? I don't like tattoos much, but I sure love what they say about people taking control of their own bodies.

That's why I like big stupid fake tits. Don't try to tell the world that you were naturally endowed like a fucking Barbie doll; let the world know that you decided you wanted a balcony someone could do Shakespeare from regardless of what god wanted. Big fake tits are a celebration of technology and humanity, and a rebellion against god and nature. I'm all for that.

Which brings us to Auto-Tune. Anyone who has heard me try to slide up to that high F on my upright bass during our show knows that I don't have a great ear. I have pretty good time, but my intonation really sucks. I've worked hard and gone from being oblivious to knowing when I'm off. The next step is to be able to figure out whether I'm sharp or flat without experimentation.

I can't sing in tune either. And now there's a gizmo that can put me right in the dead center of the note. Right in that fat middle where Sinatra and Ella always seem to be. And you can use it live too. Anthony of the Chili Peppers can now choose to be right in tune on "Under the Bridge." It's amazing technology, but I miss people being out of tune. The Monkees were produced within an inch of their lives, but if you go back and hear the records (you can still use the word "records" even for new music; it may be digital, but it's still *recorded,* don't you think? "Record" doesn't have to mean vinyl), their slightly (or more) out-of-tune harmonies give them a feeling of youth and disrespect. Lou Reed being a little flat on "Walk on the Wild Side" isn't a mistake; it evokes the pure ennui that he was living. Stevie Wonder being a little sharp cuts through that fat Sir Duke sound. Not being in tune can be a choice or a very happy accident. Now, engineers often tune stuff up reflexively, without even making a choice. You're not going to hear one of those *American Idol* fucks singing like the Go-Go's live in their own arena show, now, are you?

I miss the out-of-tune music, both the intentional and the accidental, because . . . with recorded music, the chosen and the accident become the same. They've played "Layla" so much on the radio that the out-of-tune high slide sounds perfect, and I love that. There are a lot of lo-fi musicians who are keeping things out of tune, so the battle is only lost on the cheesy Top Ten stuff, and the Top Ten is almost gone anyway. We're getting all sorts of diversity. With the cosmetic Auto-Tunes, comes the technology to do the crazy Auto-Tune. The proud 44DD of Auto-Tunes, used just for effect. I'm not sure what software the Black Eyed Peas use to sound like cartoons, but it's only one whole step from what Ross Bagdasarian used for the Chipmunks. They're not trying to fool anyone that they really sing that way. It's making a joyful noise that god never wanted us to make. I love Cher's "Believe," and I love her tattoos, but I hope she isn't trying to pass off the tits to anyone as real.

Big fake tits, tattoos, and obvious Auto-Tune feel atheist to me. All of a sudden I'm pretty happy with Fergie, and Ke$ha, and if I throw in loving anyone who is on the front lines fighting for the First Amendment, have I painted myself into a corner where I have to say that Janet Jackson is the perfect human being? I guess so. Janet does seem almost as cool as a carny pig who eats out of the trash and tattoos doodles on his ankle.

"Rock Your Body"

—Janet Jackson and Justin Timberlake at the Super Bowl

The Bible's Third Commandment

Thou shalt not take the name of the lord thy god in vain, for the lord will not hold him guiltless who takes his name in vain.

My friend Lana is a new atheist. She wrote this to me: "For me, the biggest part of letting go of god was holding myself accountable for my own actions. Life is so much easier when you think someone else is doing the deciding for you. It is easier to place blame on 'god's will' than to say 'I fucked up' or 'I need to work harder.' It felt safer to be a passenger in my own life than to take the wheel."

ONE ATHEIST'S THIRD SUGGESTION

Say what you mean, even when talking to yourself.
(What used to be an oath to god is now quite simply respecting yourself.)

Preach to Me and Pray for Me—Please!

The party line for atheists is that they don't mind religious people hanging around in polite society as long as they don't proselytize. It's okay for one to believe bugnutty shit as long as one shuts the fuck up about it. I don't agree. Proselytizing is annoying, but not proselytizing is immoral. Not proselytizing is anti-American.

I was on some Joy Behar show on CNN. There was some smart guy sitting next to me. We were talking about religion. I described myself as a "hard-core atheist." Joy and the smart guy scoffed, and Joy said mockingly, "What's a 'hard-core atheist'?"

"I don't even believe that other people believe in god."

My buddy the scientist rob pike was the first person I heard say that line. Rob didn't say it to be clever. He wasn't trying to get a laugh. It's hard to believe people believe in god. If people really believed in god, how could they ever sin? If I thought that having sex before marriage would displease an omniscient, omnipotent, omnipresent, omni-nosey power, if I really believed that, then the entire staff, male and female, on- and off-camera, every single body, of Kink.com could never have even been able to get my cock hard. What cost/benefit analysis allows one to sin? They build in that "sin in your heart" thing so that everyone feels guilty, but even with that—man, if I'm believing in the god almighty of Abraham, I can keep thoughts of Maggie Gyllenhaal bringing me coffee out of my mind (thankfully I don't have to). I don't know that anyone really *really* believes in god. Even the most faithful must feel at least the same little itch of doubt about religion that I feel about abstract painting. I love nutty art, and I know it really is great, but in the deep recesses of my mind I hear, "Maybe my four-year-old *could* do that. Maybe it really is just bullshit."

Modern art is great, it really speaks to me on an intellectual and visceral level, but there's a little stone in my shoe worrying that it might all be just jive. Anyone who believes in virgin births in a species other than lizards and other non-breasted life, anyone who believes that there's a benevolent force in the universe that cares if we jack or jill off, must be worrying in the back of his or her mind that Christ might have been just spilling random paint on the canvas about what we should be doing before we exit through the celestial gift shop. I love Stockhausen and Half Japanese, but there is a chance some of it is just noise. There's always doubt.

But let's just say that someone really believes in the life-after-death spook show and eternal life for reals. Not like I believe that Sun Ra planned exactly what the sax solos would sound like, but like I believe in gravity. They can feel it. Okay, let's go to my favorite example. This one hypothetical religious guy, let's call him Charlie Manson, really believes that "Helter Skelter" wasn't just about roller coasters and fucking. He has faith that the Beatles and/or the Bible really sent clear messages about race riots, life after death, fashion, diet, and homosexuality. If our Charlie really believed that there was everlasting life through Jesus Christ, piggies, or L. Ron Hubbard, how can he not proselytize? How can it be moral to be politely quiet about something that important? If our life here is really just a brief vale of tears and the real joy is after we croak off the mortal coil, if someone really truly believes all that like ice like fire, don't they have to preach to everyone all the time?

I don't know you from Adam, but if I saw you standing on the railroad tracks in dark clothing, in the middle of the night, right after a bend in the tracks, and I heard a train a-comin', rollin' down the track, doesn't everyone's morality mandate my saying, "Yo, there's a train a-comin', rollin' down the track—move off the goddamn tracks, stupid"?

You reply, "Shut the fuck up, you out-of-fashion, train-believing whack job, leave me alone, or I won't invite you to any cool parties." What if even while you're saying that, I feel the train a-rumblin', rollin' down the track, shaking the very ground beneath our feet, and I say, "Can't you fucking feel that? Can't you tell that you're about to be hit by a fucking train, a-comin' rollin' down the track?"

"No, leave me alone, I have a right to not believe. Richard Dawkins and Christopher Hitchens, and other really smart guys, say there's no train a-coming and these aren't even tracks. And Christ, are you really wearing a black tie and a white shirt and riding a fucking bicycle door to door? You're never going to get any pussy."

Now I can see the train, but the poor blind, deaf, numb, deluded atheist can't believe a train is a-comin', can't believe he's about to be turned into haggis. Isn't there a point when any moral person just tackles the stupid cocksucker, knocks him off the track, and saves his life? That's the only choice . . . if you really believe in that crazy imaginary train.

If someone really believes in everlasting life (that's a big, big "if," but stay with me—Jackson Pollock really is great, I love Duchamp's snow shovel, and Cage's notated silence really is music), then letting someone fuck up everlasting life is much worse than letting someone get hit by a train. Fucking up everlasting life is being hit by a train forever, and "forever" in this case is even longer than the time between when you cum and when she cums. This is like real no-kidding motherfucking forever, like dentist-drilling-into-your-teeth forever. You have to do whatever you can, even if the heathens laugh in your face and think you're worse than the stupidest of the Baldwin brothers. You can't respect someone's right to not believe in something that's going to give him or her eternal life. That's not real respect, that's callous disregard. That's negligent eternal homicide.

If you believe in everlasting life, and you keep annoying me about it, you are insufferable. Get away from me! If you believe in everlasting life and don't annoy me about it, if you're polite and let me believe what I want, even though I'm going to spend eternity in real break-is-over-back-to-the-handstands-in-the-river-of-shit hell, what kind of scumbag are you? Get away from me! How much do you have to hate someone to let that everlasting train of lost eternal life squash someone's heathen ass?

"Knock-knock."

"Who's there?"

"Atheist."

"Atheist who?"

"Oh, I'm sorry, we don't go around knocking on your door when you're trying to relax."

Atheists are also morally obligated to tell the truth as we see it. We should preach and proselytize too. We need to help believers. Someone who believes in god is wasting big parts of his or her life, holding back science and love, and giving "moral" support to dangerous extremists. If you believe something, you must share it; it's one of the ways we all learn about truth.

I made this argument for proselytizing on one of my video blogs. Proselytizing is a moral imperative and feeds the marketplace of ideas. I want to hear everyone tell the truth as they see it. I want to learn from everyone.

I'm such a fucking idiot.

That video got linked around with the fundamentalist whack jobs and I became the poster boy for evangelical crazy-ass Christians. Fuck me. They didn't just link to it on the web, but also burned it to DVDs and showed it in big megachurches all over. You could find web pages that gave you a sermon to preach around it. You read this speech, then turned it over to "famous atheist Penn Jillette" to show how important spreading the word was, and came back to pass the plate. Most of the churches just stole my video outright. They didn't ask me for my permission, and they didn't ask Sony. They just used my words to spread "the Word." I wasn't going to get involved in a lawsuit. The legal status is up in the air. But it's funny to me how few of them respected my intellectual property. More of this "end justifies the means" jive. It does, however, fill my heart with hope and joy that so many of them did respect my ideas, if not my property. Most of the showings I heard about kept in all the stuff I said about there being no god. They might have edited out a "fuck" or two, but they kept the ideas. Maybe they felt that it strengthened their case that I was an atheist, or maybe they were just doing the right thing.

The Campus Crusade for Christ was one of the groups that did everything right—you know, other than being the Campus Crusade for Christ. They wrote a nice letter to me and to Sony asking for permission to use the video. They gave me their word that they wouldn't change the context. Everyone would hear my message within their message. They would spin around it, but they'd keep my part intact. I surprised myself and some atheist friends by okaying their use of my words and image. Penn Jillette is part of the Campus Crusade for Christ. They were playing by the rules, and I like that.

That proselytizing video of mine didn't have quite the market penetration of *Dancing with the Stars*, but it was seen by millions of people. Over .0001 percent of those millions have shown up in person after the show to talk to me. They bring me Bibles and really heartfelt wishes that I'll find Christ. One man comes by our show every couple of weeks to look in my eyes, shake my hand, give me a few of his personal preaching DVDs, tell me he's off to Israel, and remind me he's praying for me. I don't know much about the Christian demographic or what keeping the Sabbath holy means, but when we took our children to the Adventuredome amusement park at Circus Circus on a Sunday afternoon, it seemed like every single mom with a stroller had seen my video in church that day. I've gotten a package of letters written by children at Christian summer camps explaining how they watched the video and are praying for me.

I'm deeply touched, saddened, disgusted, and a little freaked out by it all. I'm sent vanity-published books that write about my proselytizing video. I've become these Christians' favorite atheist. It's pathetic and annoying, but their hearts are in the right place. I believe they really care about me, and I care about these bugnutty freaky whack jobs.

My love and respect for the marketplace of ideas (that the only cure for bad speech is more speech) was reinforced by one woman who came up to me in the lobby after watching our whole show. Most of the Christian freaks don't watch our Vegas show, they just know where I'm going to be afterward and show up there to pray for me without having to give me any money. This woman hovered until the other patrons had greeted me, then told me her story. She explained that she'd seen my video at her big megachurch. She liked it. She liked it more than her church had expected her to. She did a web search and found other videos of me yapping. She said she watched them all. That little pebble of doubt in her shoe became a boulder. She wasn't calling herself a full atheist yet, but she'd quit the church and she was well on her way. She thanked me. Man, my little Grinch heart grew ten times in size. I felt like less of a dipshit for being part of the Campus Crusade for fucking Christ.

That fine lady was the only one I heard about starting down the road to atheism because of seeing my video in church. Everyone else is still praying for me, in front of computer screens and in churches all over. Part of one of the sermons built around my video includes everyone bowing their heads and praying for Penn Jillette. I have whole congregations praying for me by name. Who else has that attention who isn't on a milk carton?

So we're running a pretty good experiment. If praying does any good, it should do some good for me. People are sincerely praying for me. They're praying for me to find Christ. Is there a time frame on this? How long do I have to go Christless in Gaza before we know for sure that their praying has failed?

I haven't found Christ. I'm not even looking for him. I don't need or want salvation. I have no hope of eternal life, but I do have hope that hundreds of millions of pebbles of doubt will grow into boulders, and eventually religion will go away and people will celebrate and cherish and protect the precious life we have here now. I'll keep preaching that everywhere I can, stand on the mountain until all souls can see it, until we all agree or until all those prayers do work on me and I change my mind. And then I'll proselytize about that too.

"A Hard Rain's A-Gonna Fall"

—Bob Dylan

You Are the Model?

Penn & Teller are the guys who wear gray suits. The articles always say we wear matching gray business suits, but we've never worn matching gray business suits. The Beatles sometimes wore matching suits. The Monkees were more likely to wear clothes that were very similar but had little variations based on the different styles and personalities of Micky, Davy, Peter, and Mike. The Monkees might have worn shirts that were the same color and the same fabric, but they'd all have different collars, sleeves, cuts, and buttons. When I was a child, I thought that was so, so cool. So Teller and I wear suits that are the same color and fabric but have different cuts and linings, and we wear different shirts; sometimes I go double-breasted and Teller wears single-breasted. Some seasons the differences are subtler, but our suits never match completely.

We can't buy suits off the rack because we're different sizes, and they aren't just suits anyway—they're costumes, so we have them designed. Penn and Teller are only different sizes because of me. Most people think that Teller is little and I'm big. That's not true. Teller is normal size and I'm the different size. I'm really, really big. I'm stupidly big. I'm a fucking giant. I'm Sasquatch. I think I was too big to even be drafted into the army. At least that was going to be my argument if they hadn't abolished the draft before I turned eighteen. I'm just shy of six feet seven inches tall (if we ever go metric, I'm two meters, which is a very cool height) and my weight varies, but I try to stay twenty pounds south of three hundred. Teller is almost five feet ten. He's a normal-sized man. To give you an idea of how stupid my size is, Teller is about the same size as Art Garfunkel. Teller & Garfunkel are two regular guys; Simon & Penn are waving to each other from about the same standard deviation on opposite sides of the bell curve.

Besides our suits being very different sizes, they're all a bit tricked out. Our jacket pockets never have flaps and they're a little bigger than they should be, so it's easy to grab hidden shit and palm it. We do a lot of costume changes in the Penn & Teller show, but the audience never knows it. I have one jacket that has a breast pocket that connects through the lining to the side pocket, allowing me to place something securely in the upper pocket and then steal it from the lower pocket. I have a jacket with a big pocket on the back that Teller can sneak an American flag into. We sometimes change jackets backstage as a quick way to make sure we have the right props properly hidden in the correct pockets.

It was French magician Jean Eugène Robert-Houdin who got the idea for magicians to wear a top hat and tails—the same Robert-Houdin in whose honor Erik Weisz changed his name to Houdini. Before Robert-Houdin came along, magicians dressed like wizards or Asians (there was little difference between the two way back then). They wore conical hats and long flowing robes. The idea Robert-Houdin had was that if magicians dressed just like their audiences, the tricks would be more amazing. Magicians have been knocking off his idea for almost two hundred years without understanding it. Some magicians today still dress like they're working for audiences in nineteenth-century France. If they were working for audiences in nineteenth-century France, they wouldn't have to throw a pigeon into their tails to impress the crowd, they could just turn on a flashlight and be a god. Most magicians today dress like desperate rock stars from the mideighties. I don't understand that at all. Wouldn't they be less embarrassed in conical hats?

We understood Robert-Houdin's wardrobe idea and figured that just about every man, at some time or another, dresses in a gray suit. Maybe it's to go to work, or maybe it's as a defendant, but it's a common look. We thought it was a better idea for us than top hats and tails or baggy shirts and a wind machine. Teller and I are creepy enough; we might as well dress normal.

Our "normal" is professionally designed. One year in the nineties we were changing designers. We were going from Canali to Zegna or something. *GQ* magazine thought it would be funny to do a fashion layout on the new gray suit look for Penn & Teller. The joke was that anyone would give a fuck that our suits were changing slightly. *GQ* knows how to do fashion shoots. They set up a beautiful rooftop in Manhattan with a view of Central Park. They hired stylists for our watches and serious hair and makeup. All the cheeses from the magazine and the designer were there. It was a big fucking deal.

It was spring in NYC, and I walked from my apartment right off Times Square to the *GQ* office building. I was wearing gym shorts (with underwear; I knew I was going to be changing my clothes. I'm not modest, but I try to be polite) and a T-shirt. I don't remember what T-shirt I wore, but you can bet it was one I got for free from a radio station. Picture gym shorts with a T-shirt that says "WROK Rocks the Rockin' Rock out of Rock in the Rock City." Picture it with a pizza stain on it, even though they were catering lunch.

I don't ever brush my hair unless I'm working. It's hair that's unfashionably long. Just stupid old-man hippie hair. Recently, a woman at the Rio All-Suite Hotel and Casino sent out a message that her granddaughter was getting chemotherapy and was going to lose her hair. The Rio sent out a note asking employees with long hair to donate to Locks of Love. This group claims to make hair fungible. The little granddaughter wouldn't get my exact hair, but there would be more hair in the system, so she could get some. They cut off ten inches, and my hair is still unfashionably long. My mom tried, during much of the time our lives overlapped, to get me to cut my hair. She started when I was in junior high school, saying, "You look like a girl," and ended right before her death, saying, "You're forty-five years old. On a young man that hair was fine, but on an old man, it's really unattractive." She never gave up, but I hung tough and made sure my mom was never happy with my hair from the time I was twelve years old. For our live shows, I have microphones in my glasses. It puts the mics at just the right spot; the sound is great and it doesn't change as I move my head. It was my idea. Carl Sagan came to our show, asked me about my mics, and then started doing it; how great is that? I have battery packs on my back, and they're connected through my ponytail (Carl just had his wires hanging down his collar). It's part of mic-ing me up before the P & T show for our stage manager to work the cables through my hair, and that means she's the one who braids it, not me. When I do TV, they have hair and makeup and someone professional brushes it. I don't ever do anything with my hair. I don't even ever shave except before a show, and then only about once a week. It's not a sexy stubble like Hugh Laurie's. I have a very light beard, so it's more like some random hairs sticking out of my face here and there. I'm a fucking pig. My mother used to say I had a light beard because I was part Native American. I think it's because I have no genitals.

I showed up that day to the *GQ* offices, a little sweaty from walking, hair tangled and loose on my shoulders, in a T-shirt and dirty gym shorts. Probably exactly the way Christina Ricci shows up every day to the movie set, but very different raw material.

I went up into the office building and met the execs and the photographer and his assistants. The photo assistants were drop-dead gorgeous women; they often are. The photographer was intense in studied black casual clothing. All the magazine big cheeses were there. The metonymic term "suits" was really right for these guys. They were executive "suits" at a suit designer company. These are guys who can tie their ties better than you can jerk off. Everyone but me looked great.

Teller had a later call time than I had, so he wasn't around. They took me out on the roof and showed me the view. The photo assistants had our new gray jackets draped over their shoulders, and they were posing in the spots where we'd be standing later while the photographer took test shots to make sure the lighting and composition would be perfect for us. It might have been a joke, but it would also be a layout in *GQ*, and it was going to be perfect.

Everyone was embarrassed as they told me their makeup guy was running a bit late, but there was a whole catered spread, and if that wasn't enough, they had a gofer who could run and get me any other food I wanted. They said I should make myself comfortable, that the makeup artist would arrive presently. Our "dressing room" was a beautiful boardroom. This was *GQ* in New York City; there were no fuckups there, except me.

I didn't mind waiting. They had a few newspapers for us, so I sat down, put my feet up, and started reading the *Times*. They knew I drank caffeine-free cola, so someone brought me over a glass of that with ice.

I was on my second glass when the makeup artist arrived. He was a small, handsome, slightly effeminate man. He was dressed in shorts and a T-shirt too, but his shorts were a skintight designer take on bicycle shorts that were in fashion that year. His T-shirt was Italian and made of hummingbird-testicle flesh or something. His sunglasses cost more than his rent, and his hair and skin were perfect. He was foreign. He was Italian or something. He was swarthy. His package and makeup kit were both large and professional. He made it clear, in every way he could, that he was homosexual.

He didn't apologize for being late, even after every suit gave him the stink eye. This makeup artist was a makeup *artist*. They were lucky to have him.

One of the big cheeses asked him to get started, but an artist doesn't rush. He casually walked outside to see what it was like on the set, so that the makeup would be perfect for the shot, the way the light caught the skin. He wanted to judge how much wind there was in order to gauge his hair-care products and how much balm to put on the lips.

He sauntered back in and picked up a small piece of smoked salmon from the catered tray. No one else had dared mess it up. He ate, shrugged, and looked for somewhere he could lay out his brushes and towels.

He didn't ask where he should set up—he took over the room. This was his moment. He owned that boardroom. He commandeered the end of the dark, heavy hardwood conference table nearest the window and laid down a fresh towel. He began opening little careful latches on little careful drawers and laying out brushes.

At this moment Teller arrived. He had outdone me in the pig department. He was dressed like me, but he'd added black socks. He thought he could save some time getting dressed in the suit if he wore his black dress socks with his sneakers and shorts instead of white socks. His gym shorts were bright orange. His T-shirt was white and from JCPenney. He walked into the room, introduced himself to the suits, shook hands with the photographer, grabbed a big handful of the expensive catered food that the makeup artist had started with, shoved it in his mouth, went to the other side of the room, picked up a newspaper, and started reading, while chewing in that annoying way he does where his eyebrows move too much (we've been working together a very long time).

The makeup artist didn't even see Teller, and although he had set up right where I was sitting, he hadn't once looked at me. He was laying out brushes, palettes, differently shaped sponges, and cotton. I had put down my paper and was just watching him set up, watching him move. He knew exactly what he was doing, and I liked watching that. He was clearly great at what he did. The executives were uncomfortable with his unapologetic tardiness and slow, careful movements, and they may have projected impatience onto my observations, but I was just watching him set up.

When he was all ready, and not a fucking instant earlier, he looked up, turned in the general direction of the suits, and in his very sexy European Union accent said, "Okay, where is the model?" Please read his sentence in an accent. It doesn't matter what accent you use, but make sure it's a very heavy accent. So you can just barely understand yourself.

His whole story was in his looks and his movements, and in that sentence. This was an important gig for him career-wise (although not important enough to be on time), and more than important, it was a sexy gig for him. He was a gay man about to do a *GQ* fashion shoot. I've done some magazine and TV shoots where I know there are going to be sexy female models with us and I get very excited about going to work (although not excited enough to shave, brush my hair, and put on a clean shirt). I used to run the scenarios through my mind: this was the day I'd fall in love with another model, or, better yet, I'd bang her in the stairwell. As I sat in the *GQ* building, I imagined our makeup artist getting ready for work that day, thinking he'd be around very beautiful men. He was a very beautiful man, and, well, you never can tell, can you?

The suits answered the question "Okay, where is the model?" by pointing to me, the closest person in the room to the makeup artist in terms of geopositioning coordinates, but certainly not in terms of class, style, or taste. He looked at me, paused, and asked me, in that same generic accent you used a moment ago, "Where is the model?"

He figured they had pointed to me because I was the guy who knew where the model was. Maybe I was a . . . what the fuck could he possibly think I was? Model pointer? But whoever I was, I must have been the one who knew where the model was.

Understanding the situation, I gave him my best, most charming smile and a shrug, and I said, "I guess that's me. I guess I'm the model today."

I expected we'd share a little laugh at my expense, and then I'd say there really wasn't much he could do, so put on a little powder, brush my hair back, and we'd be done and he could move on to Teller.

That isn't what happened. He didn't back down. He looked at me like he was about to spit on me. Then he made this disgusted noise deep in the back of his throat and he said, in that intense accent, incredulously, "*You* are the mod-el?" He threw down his brush. He shook his head in disgust. Not American disgust, but that European disgust. He turned his back on me and said a simple, "No."

The designer and the *GQ* people ran across the room. The suits were moving, their ties were bouncing. They hustled him out of the room as I protested: "Hey, it's okay. It's not a big deal."

I could see them through the classy glass walls reprimanding him.

They were firing him. They were trying to figure out how they could get his makeup kit back to him without having him go back in the room. They were intense. When I'm yelled at like that, I cry. Assistants were on the phone. They were all pissed and panicked.

I didn't know what to do. I just sat there while they tore him a new attractive asshole inside his trendy bicycle shorts.

After much too long, one of the execs came in, called me "Mr. Jillette," and explained that they would get us another makeup artist. It would take about an hour, but there was another makeup artist who was very, very good and they'd called her and she could be with us in about an hour, maybe a little less. They made the feminine pronoun very clear.

I said, "No, no, no. I mean, can you blame him? No one would think I'm a model. He was caught off guard. He didn't mean anything by it. Everyone is waiting around. The light is just right in the park. Let's just use this guy and it'll be great. It's no problem. Really." They argued with me a bit, they were pissed, but it would save a lot of money to not wait around. They went out and brought him back in.

This is where this makeup man became my fucking idol. He did not apologize. He didn't even stop his European disgusted head-shake. He came over and looked at me like I was a piece of dog shit stuck to the bottom of his shoe. He hesitated before even touching me. I thought I should show him that the reason I was there was not my looks, but rather that I was funny, so I said, "I understand your disgust, it's like you're being asked to paint the *Mona Lisa* on a Big Mac." It wasn't funny or witty, but it gave him an opportunity to give me a bygones-be-bygones laugh. He didn't even smile. He never cracked a smile. He didn't even give me a "well, that's the way life goes" shrug. He touched my face like it was covered with garden slugs. My shit-eating grin, and the executives glaring, had no effect on him. He knew that my being the model was very, very wrong, and he might have to be in the room with it, but he would never condone it. I felt shame and embarrassment and I kept giggling nervously like a little girl who happened to look like an unkempt yeti, but mostly what I felt was respect. A deep respect. A deep respect like a Bob Dylan respect. Respect like the diamond bullet lodged in Colonel Kurtz's head. I was in the presence of an artist. I was in the presence of a real man.

He did my makeup and he did a fine job, but he never backed down. He didn't say a thing and he never stopped shaking his head in disgust. He finished and said, with a resignation that did not in any way blunt his dignity, "And where is the other mod-el?"

I pointed to Teller.

He buried his head in his hands.

"I'm Too Sexy"

—Right Said Fred

"I Won't Back Down"

—Tom Petty

Agnostics: No One Can Know for Sure but I Believe They're Full of Shit

"I don't have enough faith to be an atheist."

Ouch. Snap. Touché.

Sometimes that's followed by "That's why I believe in [some bullshit god]. I don't have enough faith to believe that this world could come from nothing."

Our humble atheist responds, "How did [aforementioned bullshit god] come from nothing?"

"That's beyond our understanding."

Bingo. We agree! That's what I meant when I said I was an atheist. I said that I didn't believe that anyone had the answers to existence. I don't believe the pope, John Smith, Muhammad, or even Sun Ra had an inside track to truth. I believe there's no god, like I believe that there's no Roquefort-sarsaparilla toaster pastry in my kitchen toaster oven right here, right now, in my home in Vegas. There are lots of ways I'd believe in that Toaster Strudel, but I'd like to start with something real, like smelling the motherfucker's odd Pillsbury presence wafting over me. I chose that cheese/root example carefully. I feel about god the way I feel about an imaginary Roquefort-sarsaparilla toaster pastry. It would be interesting, but I'm not sure it would be good. If you don't have enough faith to be an atheist, you certainly don't have enough faith to not be an atheist.

Ouch. Snap. Touché.

Often, "I don't have enough faith to be an atheist" is followed by "So I'm agnostic," and that pisses me off even more. "Agnostic" does not answer the theological question it pretends to answer. "Agnostic" answers an epistemological question with an answer that everyone agrees with (except the pope and me, and I'm not so sure about the pope). Thomas Huxley, Darwin's bulldog, made up the term "agnostic" in 1889:

> Agnosticism is not a creed but a method, the essence of which lies in the vigorous application of a single principle. Positively, the principle may be expressed as in matters of intellect, follow your reason as far as it can take you without other considerations. And negatively, in matters of the intellect, do not pretend that matters are certain that are not demonstrated or demonstrable.

Penn Jillette, no dogsbody, made up his own shit in 2011: "If you're not willing to pretend that matters of god can be certain, you're an atheist, and just say that, you fucking pussy."

If you're asked, "Do you think the existence of god is a matter that is demonstrable?" (I wish I got asked that question a little less often and "Would you like a blow job?" a little more often), you could start your answer with "yes" or "no." If you're self-absorbed and think that your feelings and thoughts are demonstrations, then you'd answer "yes." If you have a bit of humility you'd answer, "No, I'm agnostic." You were asked an epistemological question and you've given an epistemological answer. (To me, the question "Would you like a blow job?" is rhetorical.)

If I ask you "Do you believe in god?" the question is not general, it's specific. It's asking you to report on your thoughts. It's not "How far can your reason take you in matters of god?" it's more like "Are you hungry for some razzleberry pie right now?" It's a question about you; what do you actively believe? It doesn't matter how sure you are of your belief. It's not like you're being asked why you're hungry for razzleberry pie or if "hungry" is the same feeling to everyone, or even what the fuck a razzleberry is. None of us can really know for sure if there's a god, but belief is, if not an action, then at least a state of mind you can report on in real time. If I ask you if you believe in god, I just want to know if you have an imaginary omnipotent friend who you really believe lives outside of you in the real world. And if you don't, let's sit down and split a razzleberry pie. If you do, get off my doorstep and I'll eat my pie myself, thank you.

You know I love the answer "I don't know," I really do, and I use it whenever I can. "I don't know" is a perfectly acceptable answer to most questions (certainly for me), but not a question of what one believes. "Is there a god?" can be answered, "I don't know." "Do you believe in god?" needs to be answered yes or no, even though you haven't made up your mind for sure. None of us has made up our mind for sure, but what are you thinking now? You don't have to know if you're always going to want a piece of razzleberry pie, just whether you want one now.

If you answer a personal question about belief with an epistemological answer, you'll get away with it pretty often. It's a cheesy grade-school dodge, and those often work ("I know you are, but what am I?"). It's a transparent trick that'll make you more comfortable at shallow cocktail parties that no one should be comfortable at anyway. It's saying that when it comes to the most important fucking decision a human being can make, you'd rather not say. Imagine trying that weasel agnostic answer in any other important discussion. The conversation would have to go like this:

"Do you believe the Velvet Underground was the best rock musical ensemble that ever made noise on planet Earth?"

"Well, I'm not sure we can ever know for sure who the best musicians are, or even what rock music is. I'm not sure anyone can know that."

"I didn't ask you that, you Grateful Dead–loving piece of dope-damaged wishy-wash, I asked you what *you* believed. But don't even bother. I no longer care. Go listen to Lady Antebellum."

I try to stay calm about theology, but I can't do it with the Velvets. I get worked up.

"Agnostic" is often peddled as the gentler, more measured version of atheist, but I can't see it that way. It doesn't fool anyone. When someone hedges, we all know what he or she means. Most "agnostics" are really just cowardly and manipulative atheists. What "agnostic" means in this context is: "Well, I don't actively believe in a god, but I can't prove there isn't one, and I'll probably break down and pray when I get really sick to attempt to fool the possible god, and you might be religious, and you are kind of cute; maybe your next question is going to be about a blow job, and I don't want to fuck that up."

"Agnostics" are not really showing respect for religious people, they're showing condescension. They worry anyone who believes in god can't possibly respect someone else's honest lack of belief. That's not true. I meet religious people every day who don't kill people for their lack of belief. Some of them will even blow you. The people listening to your answer know you're human and can change your mind. They know you can be wrong. I say I'm atheist now, but that doesn't mean my next book won't be titled *God? Yes!* We all change. Do "agnostic" weasels think that they can manipulate the believer with their fancy wordplay? Do they think that they'll dazzle the faithful with phony nonjudgmental compassion and undermine their faith from a gentle nonconfrontational position? Religious people aren't as stupid as "agnostics" think (no one could be). Believers can smell a godless loser who doesn't even have the guts to answer a question from half the length of purgatory away. An outright lie shows more respect than a dodge. If you're going to lie, get down on your knees, pretend to praise god, and rot the faith from the inside like the worm that you are.

Believers and "agnostics" sometimes try to claim that atheists are arrogant, sad assholes who believe science has answered all the questions of existence. I have never heard an atheist claim anything like that. I read all the Hitchens/Harris/Dawkins/Dennett stuff and bunches of flaming "fuck god" websites, and I just don't see that claim anywhere. It's not arrogant to say that you can't figure out the answers to the universe with your internal faith. It's not arrogant to know that there's no omniscient, omnipotent prime mover in the universe who loves you personally. It's not sad to feel that life and the love of your real friends and family is more than enough to make life worth living. Isn't it much sadder to feel that there is a more important love required than the love of the people who have chosen to spend their limited time with you? When someone says that Jesus loves them, it's always so sad and desperate. If your Christ lives outside of time, then the time he takes to love you means nothing, and anyway, why did he make your football team lose?

Here's hoping the faithful will find real people who'll love them half as much as I feel loved by my family and friends. And I can show you my family and friends in person—I can prove they exist; you don't have to take it on faith. While we're waiting for my buddies to get here, wanna see some pictures of my family on my iPhone? I have 616 photos here, and a few videos, c'mon, it'll only take a minute—aren't they the best?!

I will keep saying and writing this over and over: the vast majority of human beings are good. We're all trying to figure out the truth. We all need more information and we can all handle your personal opinion when we ask for it. Please respect us enough to tell the truth as you see it. Just spit it out. Most of us will be happy to hear what you have to say. That's most of us. Some of us will kill you for what you believe—but with those people, "agnostic" won't save your ass. And it sure won't get you laid.

I am an atheist.

"Jesus"

—The Velvet Underground

The Bible's Fourth Commandment

Remember the Sabbath day, to keep it holy. Six days thou shalt labor and do all thy work, but the seventh day is the Sabbath of the lord thy god. In it thou shalt do no work: thou, nor thy son, nor thy daughter, nor thy manservant, nor thy maidservant, nor thy cattle, nor thy stranger who is within thy gates. For in six days the lord made the heavens and the earth, the sea, and all that is in them, and rested on the seventh day. Therefore the lord blessed the Sabbath day and hallowed it.

I went into a hotel room with a girlfriend. I told her I was very sorry, but I had a little bit of writing that I had to do before I could take her out to dinner. I said it would take about an hour.

I said, "You can turn on the TV; my iPod has music on it and there are headphones right there. If you want to go out, my car keys are right there and there's a Starbucks in the lobby. I have a couple books there if you want to read and there's a magazine or two . . ."

She said, "I'm fine, I'll just sit here."

"What are you going to do?" I asked.

"I'll sit and think."

She's still one of my best friends and an inspiration.

ONE ATHEIST'S FOURTH SUGGESTION

Put aside some time to rest and think. (If you're religious, that might be the Sabbath; if you're a Vegas magician, that'll be the day with the lowest grosses.)

Learning to Fly, Strip, and Vomit on a 727

Since I was a child, I've wanted to be weightless. I really wanted to go to space, but part of going to space was being weightless. Just to hold something up in front of me and have it stay right there is the real magic. It's out of this world. I have professionally battled gravity. My start in showbiz was as a juggler. Jugglers fight gravity. "Sudden gust of gravity" is the standard (meaning they've forgotten who they stole it from) line that hack jugglers use as they bend over looking like they're chasing a duck after they've dropped a prop. The reason there aren't any superstar jugglers is because no matter how good you get, at some point you're onstage looking like you're chasing a duck.

Elvis never looked like he was chasing a duck. Hendrix never looked like he was chasing a duck. John Lennon never looked like he was chasing a duck. I've often looked like I was chasing a duck.

Now that I'm older and weigh 280 pounds, gravity is a less sporting and more real enemy. As you know, I'm six feet seven inches tall, and I still remember Leslie Fiedler writing in *Freaks: Myths and Images of the Secret Self* that "gravity is not kind to those who grow too large." I would be healthier (and more lucrative) if I were built like Tom Cruise.

A good theory in science is one that we're damn sure is true: the

Earth goes around the sun. Evolution is how we got here. No one I know seriously doubts those. But no one has the full skinny on gravity.

The only way you can feel weightless for more than a couple of roller-coaster seconds is by getting far enough away from Earth or riding the Vomit Comet. The Vomit Comet is how NASA trains astronauts and rich people thrill important clients. They take a big old airplane and they go up and down really fast. While you're going up, you weigh 1.8 times your weight, and while you're going down, you weigh around 0.

Up until recently, the FAA had given NASA a monopoly on losing all your pounds of ugly fat (along with muscle, bone, and everything else). Astronauts got to ride it, some scientists got to ride it, and that's about it. Ron Howard made some back-room deal (it *must* have included sexual favors) to be able to shoot *Apollo 13* on the NASA Vomit Comet and they talked about it a bit, but it was soon quieted down. You're not really supposed to use a government-funded program to make movies. I'm glad Tom, Bill, and Kevin got to fly, but if everyone really thought about it, why can't we all ride?

More and more people are getting a chance to be weightless. A couple free-market nuts at NASA decided they loved zero G and it was time to get off the socialist tit, buy their own Vomit Comet, and start selling rides on it. Everything the Vomit Comet does is within the specs of planes, and why can't at least rich people get to do what Ron and Tom got to do? That was the idea.

When they first got this harebrained scheme, before it had been approved by the FAA or whoever, I heard about it. It seems that when anyone gets a harebrained scheme, I'm CC'd on the memo. I love nuts, I'm for nuts, I am nuts. They all get in touch with me. I told them I thought it was a great idea (and you know how much that means), and I wrote them e-mail, gave them tickets to our show, and went to dinner with them a couple times.

Several years ago, while they were still working on getting approval to fly civilians, they figured out how I could go up in their Vomit Comet: they'd make me an employee of their company, Zero G. I'd go up in one of the flights they were conducting to train their pilots how to best hit zero G. My six years of grueling cheerleading had paid off: I was going to be weightless.

It was not without price. I had to get up early. We'd been working hard on a TV show and I needed a rest, but I got up early in Vegas and caught the 8:10 to Burbank. Getting up wasn't hard. I was as excited as a little kid and didn't sleep anyway. I decided to have a Cinnabon ("You pig!") for breakfast because I thought it might taste nice coming back up. It *is* called the Vomit Comet. I slept the whole flight to Burbank and went from Burbank to Van Nuys by car. At the airport I ran into another Zero G "employee," Billy Gibbons (yup, from ZZ Top). Billy's also a guy who cheerleads for nuts. Look at us, for Christ's sake. The Zero G boys had run into Billy at an airport somewhere and had invited him along too.

On board would be two pilots, the four guys who were working on starting the company, a flight doctor, a nurse, and two paramedics. One of the NASA guys brought his girlfriend (another "employee"), a platinum blonde with way-big aftermarket breasts. I've always wanted to fuck in zero G, and the aftermarket-breasted girlfriend of someone else was my first choice. I tried to make a case that these were extraordinary circumstances and her boyfriend, who was busy doing airplane stuff, would be fine with us fucking for science, but she didn't go for it. She thought I was trying to ask her out for another time. I wasn't trying to ask her out; I didn't want to date her, I wanted to fuck someone in zero G, and she was a better choice than the officious medical people and Billy. Mary Roach, the great writer, also did a Zero G flight and tried to bring her husband up to fuck her. I wish we had been on the same flight. I could have tried dressing up like her husband. When the busty blonde said no, I winked at Billy, but he was also a no-go.

Billy was big as life, with his big old Warner Bros. cartoon hillbilly beard, an African hat, a $250,000 Gibson starburst guitar, a six-pack of beer, and a specially made amp that had been built inside a can of peanuts. He looked great. Billy is thin. Shaved, he would weigh about a hundred pounds. He was beaming all over. I've known Billy about twenty-five years, and although we don't see each other much, he feels like a friend—not enough of a friend to have sex with me in zero G, but a good friend all the same. We were ready to go.

We walked out on the runway, and there was the mystical plane that would battle gravity for us. It was a beat-up 727 cargo plane that read MEXICARGO on the side. Oh, my word. I'm not one to engage a lot in ethnic humor, but I did have to have some fun talking to Billy about our lives riding on "beans and Bondo." Man, it looked jury-rigged and fly-by-night. But we were ready.

I was intent on exploring the science behind *Barbarella.* I asked one of the owner guys to run a little video camera for me—I wanted to get some video comparing Hanoi Jane's strip in zero G, which of course had been faked by having her lie on glass, with a *real* strip in zero G by me. I was going to go weightless and strip naked. The blonde really wanted to join me, and I thought it would help the science, but her boyfriend said he thought her stripping would hurt Zero G's credibility with the FAA. Big guys stripping in space is serious research.

Anyway, inside, the plane was mostly a lot of big open space. At the back were three rows of old coach seats with oxygen bottles just lying on them, a cooler tied down with ropes, a box of Ziplocs that would be used for our vomit, and a big mat on the floor. An astronaut guy did a little flight attendant speech, except we all really listened. This wasn't some food server in the sky; this was a real former NASA guy. "We have lost cabin pressure a few times," he told us, "so we might have to use the oxygen." In the event we needed the oxygen, it wasn't going to drop down and turn on—we would have to find it and turn on the oxygen from the bottle. Of course, if we did lose cabin pressure we'd be heading down to thicker air so fast we wouldn't have time for the oxygen before we were safe (or dead), but our guy was having fun scaring us. The Vomit Comet, for all the weirdness, is safe. It's doing safe stuff. It's as safe as any big plane, and that's safer than hanging out on your front steps. It just doesn't seem safe, and for creeps like us, that adds to the fun.

Now here is how weightlessness works: this huge plane does parabolas. It goes pretty close to straight up for thirty seconds, and then it turns around and heads straight for the ocean. You know that feeling you get at the top of a roller coaster before the big drop, that feeling where your stomach goes to your throat? On a coaster it'll last a second or so. Well, this plane becomes a huge roller coaster, and instead of a second you get thirty seconds. Thirty seconds of that feeling. The roller coaster example doesn't tell you anything. Thirty seconds of Vomit Comet weightlessness is not sixty times a half second of Six Flags weightlessness. It's a different thing. Imagine an hourlong orgasm. You can't—and that's my point.

Another way to look at how it works is that we're falling straight down and the plane, and everyone else, and even the air, is staying around us in the same relative position. It's not easy for the pilots. They're flying straight down at the water, and they're trying to keep the plane heading perfectly straight down, and then they pull out, and back up you go, and when you go back up, you go to 1.8 G. I would go from weightless to 504 pounds in a few seconds. We would go from 0 G to 1.8 G and we were going to do it over thirty times! We would be weightless for at least fifteen minutes altogether. That would be longer than Alan Shepard on his first flight.

I would also weigh 504 pounds for 15 minutes. It wasn't the zero G that would make us vomit, it was the 1.8 G. At the end of each zero G segment we'd hear the call "Thirty seconds!" and have to quickly sit down and get our heads straight up, perpendicular to the floor. It would be better if we didn't talk or laugh or look around, but just sit. That was our best chance of not getting sick. And we would have no idea where we were. The plane has only one small window in the middle of the open space. It's recessed and hard to look through. We wouldn't be able to sync our eyes with what our bodies were feeling. Like a roller coaster in the dark with no wind. Everything would be moving with us. We would just feel it in our bodies.

It's very weird to be in an airplane unable to see out any windows. I mean, when you sit on the aisle, you may not think you're seeing out the windows, but it's so odd when you really can't. We took off and then had to fly out over the ocean, and it took a while with all the noise regulations over Southern California. Finally, it was time. We'd do "two

Martians, two lunars, and then go to zero." That meant we'd have two thirty-second legs at one-third gravity, two at one-sixth gravity, and then the real deal. In between each one, we'd get heavy. They told us we might want to stay in our seats for the first few until we got used to it. Billy and I were told to start slow; if we felt sick, we should come back to the seats and strap in, and they'd be there to help us. As we began the first leg—the first "Martian"—the NASA guy used his arm to illustrate the orientation of the plane, so we could understand a little of what we were feeling. We were told to be careful, but the real boys were walking around, even during the going-up times. His arm sloped up and I felt heavy. I mean I was really pushed into my seat, and then . . . his hand . . . as I stared at his arm curving, I felt lighter.

I was lighter. The pros started dancing and jumping. I had to shake my head. They were moving in slow motion. I had seen this motion in movies, but I had never actually *witnessed* it. They're both stocky men, but now they were jumping huge distances, doing backflips together and landing on their feet. I felt my arms; they were so light. And then we got heavy. I could feel the skin of my face pull down, and it was hard to lift my arms. That lasted thirty seconds, and then we started another Martian.

Billy couldn't wait; he was up out of his seat, jumping and giving a Texas "Woooo!" I was a little more cautious; I unbuckled and lifted myself from my seat. I was a gymnast. I could hold my whole weight with my arms with no strain. Man oh man. "Thirty seconds!" came the call, and we got heavy. I was back in my seat, looking straight up, trying not to get sick. But I was doing fine. Okay, on lunar, I would rock.

The angle of Bob's arm told us it was coming, and we were lunar. Weighing forty-seven pounds, I jumped into the big empty space with the mat on the floor, very cautiously. I went right to the ceiling (not far for me). I've always wanted to walk on my hands, and there I was, like the greatest circus star you've ever seen, running along on my palms. Billy was dancing some weird ZZ Top/Texan nut dance. The busty girlfriend was doing cartwheels and flips. The medical people were just getting up out of their seats. "Thirty seconds!" we were warned, and

I hurried to the edge of the plane and sat on the floor with my head straight up, really feeling the weight this time.

My second lunar was great. My handstand was better, and I tried a flip. I fell over, but it felt great. I was so strong. The body that I've been stuck in for decades became new. I was stronger. Looking at the others was amazing. It really was slow motion. I had never even seen what I was seeing, let alone felt it! Amazing. I stood on one hand. I spun and flew. "Thirty seconds!" And I rushed to the wall, and felt the oppressive weight come back almost double. Time to pay the piper.

Now it was straight up and down. The heavy was really heavy, but soon we were going to be weightless. I sat straight and quiet and waited. It was a long thirty seconds of gravity oppression, and then, the tilt of the arm—and freedom, complete freedom. I pushed off and, still seated, floated in the air. Billy came flying at me and I caught him. There was no up or down; I was upside-down and I had military NASA ass over my head. I grabbed the girlfriend and tossed her lightly to Billy. When she got to Billy they both went off together. Someone grabbed me and spun me around.

"Thirty seconds!"

Like a ton of bricks. I scrambled to the wall. I breathed through my nose. I lifted my arms and it took all I had. I could feel my stomach, and my head was hard to hold up. This was only 1.8 G, but thirty seconds is a long time.

Weightless again. Billy and I were laughing, hugging, and floating. I did all the stuff I remembered seeing astronauts doing. I got myself spinning in one place in a little ball. Up and down didn't matter. We were all bumping into each other. Well, wait a minute, not all. Billy and I looked over at the cocky medical team. All but one of them were in their fancy scrubs, still seat-belted in, vomiting their guts out in sheer misery. I don't know if they had even stood up. It was going to be a *very* long two-hour flight for them. They weren't going to be there to help us. I said to Billy, "Yeah, flight doctors aren't ready for this. But the old road dogs can do anything—we've played Cleveland!" Billy got to laughing, spinning in space with his stupid hat, hillbilly beard, voodoo necklaces, and tight rocker jeans, yelling, "We've played Cincinnati!" (He changed it.) It was wild.

"Thirty seconds!"

I wasn't quite sitting down, just kind of hovering near the side of the plane, and I slid down the wall as the next heavy leg began. They had told me to keep my head up, so I fought—man did I fight—and I got to a sitting position, and I tried to breathe slowly and remember it would be over soon. We were weightless over and over: I got into a full-lotus yoga position and floated around. Billy liked that, and then next time he did it too. We sat next to each other like gurus and got all ready—we took off together and floated by the video camera. I found myself on top of Billy as "Thirty seconds!" came and had to use all my strength to not crush him. The same thing happened later with the girlfriend, and I used a little less of my strength and crushed her a little just for fun. She was fun to be on top of.

It was time to get to work. Billy went first: he got out his guitar, this beautiful Gibson that he'd borrowed for this flight. The NASA guys didn't sit down at 1.8, they walked around. Nothing changed for them, except how they moved. They went back and forth from flying to trudging, but they were over helping the vomiting medics, shooting the video for Billy, and running up and talking to the pilots. These guys were used to it. So they got Billy's guitar out and they shot some rock video stuff. I tried to stay out of the shot, but as he was spinning the guitar, ZZ style, in front of him, he lost control and I had to catch it. The other novice, the blonde, was trying to get into the shots. It looked great. The beard flying, the necklaces flying, and the guitar just floating.

I played around with a ball; it would just float in front of me. Amazing. And even more amazing was tossing the ball in 1.8, because you've never seen *that* in movies. There's no way to fake it. Throwing it hard, I couldn't hit the ceiling. Throwing and catching the one ball wasn't easy. Amazing. I want to try to juggle three in 1.8. It would take some time.

Billy had gotten the video test that he wanted, and it was time for me to work. I was going to strip like Jane Fonda in *Barbarella.* We had been back and forth a lot of times and I was getting beads of sweat on my forehead and it was getting tough. The rich guys who do it now are doing fifteen parabolas maximum, and we'd already done twenty. I was getting a little panicky, but it was time for the real wildness.

I told everyone that I was going all the way, that I would be naked. I let my hair down and it flew better than Jane's. I licked my lips. We went 0 G and I tried to work the camera and lick my lips and play the eyes and get my hands in my hair. I sexily unlaced my big old size 15 Doc Marten and let it float, with my sock, in front of me. Man, it looked great.

I couldn't do the whole strip in thirty seconds, and even in hunks of zero G it would take too long, so I had to keep stripping in 1.8. Man, that was hard, but I got my other boot off. Everything I removed the NASA boys had to grab and tie down so it wouldn't hurt anyone. I undid my belt, played with it stripper style, and let it go to float like a sea snake. Next were the pants, and those came off while I twirled in a ball. In a few thirty-second hunks, I was down to T-shirt and boxers. I whipped the shirt off and then tried for a move I was really hoping would work. I pushed off the wall so I would be spinning, and I took off my boxers as I floated toward the camera. I timed it right; it was perfect: as I took them off my ass hit the camera.

Now I was in zero G and naked! I was free, the first person to be naked on the Vomit Comet. (If you have the desire to see me naked in zero G, first of all, I'm flattered, and second, you can see it: we showed a clip on one of the *Penn & Teller: Bullshit!* shows on Showtime, and the clip is on YouTube, so if you want to see it, go ahead. And thank you.) Seeing me floating around naked, the NASA guys had to prove they weren't gay. "It's the first time I've been nauseous in zero G!" one said, and the one with the camera panned back and forth between me naked and the medics throwing up.

The next few times, I was just going wild. I put my hands over my package and went spinning on my axis. I was trying to cover my dick and balls and do all the sexy Jane faces—Jane was coy, and I had to be too. This was science, this was the *Barbarella* project. With my arms being used to cover my cock and balls, navigation was tough.

I inspired the NASA guy's girlfriend (I don't like calling her that, but I want to respect her privacy). She had been told she couldn't strip, but as I sat across from her in 1.8, she lifted up her shirt. In 1.8 gravity, her saline bags did not even bend. Man, that's some nutty surgery. Those huge tits didn't even feel the 1.8. Wow. I think she was starting to understand that maybe we could fuck for science, but there was no time for me to work her. I had plans, while she was taking her shirt off, to spin around naked. The video guy didn't know what to cover. He knew he should cover me, and he wanted to cover her.

Well, as I was spinning, and she was starting to strip, we got a gust of negative G that threw us to the ceiling. I was rolling, naked, across the ceiling, and then the thirty seconds were up, and I was back on the floor rolling. As I went by, I hit my belt and saw that my dad's silver dollar was gone from the buckle, the silver dollar my dad had given me. He had just died. Dad had worn that silver dollar belt buckle all his adult life and now it was mine. I was really worried. I yelled, "Find the silver dollar, please!" I thought I was going to cry. I should have known that the fuselage was closed and I couldn't lose it, but I was naked and confused. NASA had no trouble finding my coin, but in all the excitement—of being naked, being bumped around, huge breasts whacking the ceiling, and just worrying about the belt buckle—I didn't get myself to a nice seated position by the time 1.8 came around, and I couldn't get my orientation. I couldn't get it together. I was dizzy from spinning (that axis thing is an advanced move), and, *bam,* did I feel sick.

"Man, I'm going to be sick."

NASA got me a bag, and I leaned over into it and started vomiting. It really hurt the muscles in 1.8; then we went weightless, and I panicked a little. The video guy said, "I've got you, don't worry about anything." He held my arm as I floated, naked and vomiting. He told me later he kept the camera on me while I floated naked and vomited into my hair, the bag, and all over him and myself. Sexy! Actually, I didn't really vomit on myself or him. The vomit just floated there in 0 G, then it went to 1.8 vomit and landed all over us. Heavy vomit.

NASA was all over me with paper towels, and they really cleaned me up. I don't like to vomit, but I've heard on heroin you vomit and don't care. This was like that. I didn't care much. Also, this wasn't flu-bile-pizza vomit. This was friendly caffeine-free-Diet-Coke-and-bits-of-Cinnabon, we're-having-fun vomit. Billy had almost vomited a while before and was staying cool. He didn't vomit. The problem was that I got a little nauseated and then did all this stupid stuff for the camera.

After I was cleaned up, I put on my boxers in 1.8 and felt mostly better. We only had a couple of zeros left and I enjoyed them quietly. I really enjoyed them. I floated in my boxers. The girlfriend gave up on getting her top off; she was never able to do it—it takes a man to strip in space.

We were done and had to fly all the way back to the airport. It was about an hourlong flight. I was uncomfortable but elated. I sat down next to the vomiting medics (great name for a band), who hadn't had any fun, and I talked to one of the NASA guys about having spent his first two days in space really, really sick. They said I was over the worst, and next time up even the 1.8 wouldn't bother me much. My whole body was different. Every time the plane took a little dip, I got ready to lift off. Man, my body knew what it was to fly and I couldn't let that go.

It was a long flight back to base. I came off the plane in my boxers. I got dressed. I didn't know what I was feeling. I wasn't even excited. As Billy said, I had to "get back my sea legs." I didn't know what to feel.

Billy, the NASA guys, and I went to a Mexican bar and restaurant. I was hungry. Throwing up in your hair gives you a hell of an appetite. We talked. I pitched an idea for the Zero G ZZ Top/P & T video to Billy, thinking we needed to find some way to do this again. We talked about how to get the Zero G guys to make a ton of money off this and how to get through the rest of the red tape that had already held them up for six years. I see they're selling rides now, so I guess they solved it, and I hope they're making money. Billy and I never did the video, but we'll share that day forever. He calls me once in a while and there's that special bond you have with a guy who's played guitar while you've floated around naked in zero G.

After four hours in the bar I got a lift to the real airport and flew back to Vegas. I slept on the flight, and every time there was a little bump, my arms went to the arms of the chair, and I was ready to push off and fly.

In bed that night I could feel myself getting light. I was sore and tired the next day, but every ten minutes or so I would feel like I was able to spin in the middle of the room. And even today, just sitting here, I have the feeling that I might be able to just float away.

My body has learned that it can fly.

"Tush"

—ZZ Top

Supreme Court Justice Ron Jeremy

I live in a nutty house. We call it the Slammer. It looks like a prison. It's very industrial, lots of concrete and chain link, but it's not called the Slammer because it looks like a correctional facility or because my dad was a jail guard. It's called the Slammer after the groovy quarantine facility at USAMRIID, the United States Army Medical Research Institute for Infectious Diseases, at Fort Detrick in Maryland. USAMRIID's stated purpose is "to conduct basic and applied research on biological threats resulting in medical solutions to protect the warfighter." Cool!

Around the time I was moving from New York City to Las Vegas (when you're doing Off-Broadway and Broadway in New York City, and you tell your peers that you're moving your show to Vegas, it's a little like being a New York City fine artist and telling everyone in SoHo that from now on your media will be fluorescent paints on black velvet and your subjects will be exclusively Elvis Presley and Jesus Christ sweating and crying, respectively and vice versa), we did a Penn & Teller run at the Capitol Theatre in Washington, DC. In that show I had a broken-bottle juggling routine that was about thirty seconds of juggling broken liquor bottles and fourteen minutes of monologue that rambled a bit, like this book. During that monologue I talked about how the audience didn't have the proper sympathy for me. They didn't have enough empathy to fear my getting hurt juggling the impossibly difficult, jagged glass bottles. I told them, "Even if I were to dip these bottles in fresh Ebola Zaire virus, cut myself, come down with hemorrhagic fever onstage, and have my eyeballs pop, most of you would turn to the person next to you and say, 'I hope Teller doesn't catch it, he's kinda cute.' "

The big cheese from USAMRIID was at the gig that night, and my hemorrhagic fever reference suggested to him that I might be interested in a tour of his facility. He allowed me to invite our crew to join us for the tour, and most of them did. It's still the most P & T crew members who have ever shown up for a field trip. When we were all invited to see U2, I could get only my manager and my wife to come along. With the USAMRIID tour, our guys had found what they were looking for.

The tour was amazing. I wanted to sign up to do some "guinea pigging," which is being used as a test subject to see how people react to catching a certain virus. It would be a way for me to help people without having to do any work. I could sit in a room, read, and have blood drawn every few hours. They wouldn't let me do it.

We learned a lot on the tour and saw a lot. I looked through the thick glass of the negative-air-pressured room at the woman who works with airborne, fatal, incurable diseases all day long. We flirted, as best we could, through the glass. I found her intact airtight positive-pressure suit so sexy. It was the kind of suit Dustin Hoffman wears in *Outbreak.* That movie was bullshit, of course, but I would have loved to watch it with the cats and kitties from USAMRIID. It would be like watching *Silence of the Lambs* with Jeffrey Dahmer. You got to hand it to Dustin Hoffman; you have to be a pretty serious actor to look like Dustin and wear that stupid hat with a magnifying glass over your nose. The USAMRIID woman in the serious infectious disease room filled out the crucial bunny suit very nicely, and I found her job so sexy. This is a woman with some serious balls. So sexy. She's not going to worry about that little cold sore on your lip before she kisses you. I never got to talk to her, though; it took her too long to get through the showers, so she couldn't greet tour guests.

Right after I watched Ms. Ebola in her room, our host showed us "the Slammer." It was a room that *nothing* went out of; every molecule of air was treated. If Ms. Groovy Diseases had ripped her suit on a broken infected monkey tibia, she'd have been rushed into this room for extreme quarantine and kept there until she died. I had been working on Broadway and doing TV for a while, and I thought that my Fortress of Solitude should be extreme quarantine, a place where I could stay until I died. As I began to plan my house, I decided to call it the Slammer, and the name stuck.

I built most of the Slammer before I had even met my wife or thought about having children. It's like it was designed by a twelve-year-old boy with a lot of money and no legal guardian. There's a fire pole coming down from my office to the courtyard. There are secret rooms behind bookcases (so much for secret, but there are others too). There was a sex dungeon off the bedroom that has since been turned into a nursery (the wonderful story of my life). My office has a urinal and a sink (I still don't know why you need both), there's a band room with rock and roll and jazz instruments set up all the time, and there's a big home theater. All this, and it looks like an industrial complex with real human skeletons hanging here and there. When it was being built, the only real grown-up in my life was my business manager, and he worried about the Slammer's resale value. "No one is going to want to spend money to buy Penn Jillette's house. You're not Elvis. It's not Graceland. So you're killing your resale value by making it this crazy. Put in marble floors or tile or something expensive to misdirect from the fire pole."

While I was ignoring my business manager's expensive advice, my senior adviser, LOD, whom I don't pay at all, was in Vegas visiting. Lawrence O'Donnell Jr. was Senator Daniel Patrick Moynihan's senior adviser, a big-cheese writer on *The West Wing*, and now host of *The Last Word with Lawrence O'Donnell* on Fox News Channel (just kidding, it's on MSNBC). We've been friends forever, and I go to him for advice.

I was telling LOD about some sort of Halloween fetish ball that I'd just been to. Someone had taken pictures of me with some very attractive women who were not dressed for climbing Everest. I don't do drugs, and I don't drink, but I still enjoyed this shindig. I asked LOD if I should be worried about the pictures showing up in the future.

LOD went into a flattering speech about how he personally thought that I would make a pretty good Supreme Court justice. The Constitution said nothing about needing a law degree or even being smart. LOD thought I'd do a good job and look cool in the robes. "But," he said, "it isn't going to happen. No one is going to offer you a position on the Supreme Court, so you don't need to worry about the pictures showing up at the confirmation hearings. You're a fucking juggler! Who cares? It's like your house, the so-called Slammer; you're never going to be able to sell it anyway. But you don't need to sell it, so don't worry about resale value. Accept who you are and do whatever you want."

I found that when I stopped lying to myself and stopped planning for futures that weren't going to happen, I got happier. It was easy. I like that my door to the Supreme Court was slammed in my face. I liked realizing that it would be okay to shave my eyebrows and replace them with calligraphy tattoos of "fuck" over the right eye and "you" over the left eye.

I was taken with these thoughts, and I was preaching this new freedom. My girlfriend at the time was quite taken with the idea as well. She was an actress, and she found it liberating to think that she didn't have to worry at all about whether she showed her tits in movies or not. Who cared? She wasn't going to be on the Supreme Court. (She still hasn't shown her tits in a movie; she married some guy and got knocked up, and I still see her pop up grieving on police shows, but I've never seen her tits on TV. I don't know if she still thinks about it, since like a few ex-girlfriends, she doesn't talk to me much anymore.)

Besides convincing this woman she was never going to be on the Supreme Court, and giving her a party with a cigarette-smoking monkey in a diaper that she could laugh at (in some ways I was a pretty good boyfriend), I also introduced her to Ron Jeremy (make your own call as to whether that introduction is "good boyfriend" or "bad boyfriend").

Ron Jeremy is not a porn star, he is *the* porn star. He will show his big dick to anyone. He's not all that attractive and never was all that attractive. He's older than you by a lot and he still gets paid to fuck. If that's not the American dream, I'm a self-fellating blue-nosed gopher. I have gone out in public with Debbie Harry, Jay Leno, Madonna, and Johnny Depp. None of them gets the same attention or is as recognized as Ron Jeremy. It's amazing; guys will knock over naked porn women just to get near Ron. He's a superstar.

I introduced my girlfriend to Ron Jeremy, and a few weeks later they got together with some other people for lunch. I wasn't there. Ron was discussing some decisions he was making. I can't even make up an example of what those might be. My girlfriend decided it was the perfect time to share the new LOD wisdom with Ron and the gang. "Don't worry about it, Ron. You're not going to be nominated for the Supreme Court; these choices will not be revisited in your confirmation hearings."

She said Ron froze. He didn't know what to say. He was heartbroken and angry. "What? You can't know that. You can't say I have no chance of being on the Supreme Court."

She hung tough. "Yes, I can. We all can."

"No, I could be on the Supreme Court."

"You've made over a thousand pornographic movies. You blew yourself on camera for money—repeatedly," she reminded him.

"But you can't say that I wouldn't be on the Supreme Court. You can't say that for sure."

He is right. We can't say that for sure. We really can't.

I read something Thelonious Monk wrote for his band members, rules they should follow about his music and art in general. One of them was, "The genius is the one who is most like himself."

LOD's advice was a cheap shortcut. It's easier to be yourself once you decide you have no chance of being on the Supreme Court. The genius way to be yourself is to accept that you might be on the Supreme

Court and still star in movies where you blow yourself. That's the real genius.

It's very, very unlikely that we'll have Supreme Court Justice Ron Jeremy. Extremely unlikely. But not impossible.

And if we do . . . oh man, we'll all be geniuses.

"You Sexy Thing"

—Hot Chocolate

I Also Couldn't Get Laid in a Women's Prison with a Fistful of Pardons

I spent several hours one Sunday evening in 1981 in the Club Baths, a gay bathhouse in San Francisco. I'm nervous and uncomfortable writing the story of that night, not because I had gay sex in public, and not because I couldn't have gay sex in public. It was a wonderful night full of many emotions and a lot of laughing, and I was embarrassed then, but I'm not ashamed now. I'm cautious because of all the sadness that must be associated with that time and place. I don't remember the exact date of my visit, but it was a Sunday in 1981. Any Sunday in 1981 was a bad time to have enjoyed a gay bathhouse. In June of 1980, flight attendant Gaëtan Dugas was diagnosed with Kaposi's sarcoma. He would continue flying cheaply around the world, having lots of unprotected gay sex. He did much of his fucking in bathhouses. The legend and myth is that he was "patient zero" (from a misunderstanding of a CDC paper that dubbed him "patient O" for "Out of California"). Dugas had a zillion sex partners, and would even tell some of them after sex that he had "the gay cancer" and maybe now they would get it too. Gaëtan went to the Club Baths in San Francisco in 1981. I don't know the dates he was there and I don't know the date I was there, but there were a lot of people fixing to die whenever I had my little night of gay exploration.

I'm going to change some of the names of the main characters in this story. My girlfriend at this time was Tracy. I'm still friends with her, and she's still just as wonderful, and she's happy for me to use her name. But I'm going to call my "breeder friend" "Bernard" because I've fallen out of touch with him, and I don't want to connect again to get his okay. I don't feel like talking to him about twenty years of not talking. Most of the sex at the Club Baths was anonymous and most of the other people in this story are anonymous. I'm going to call my "gay friend," the star of this story, "Charles," because I don't want to hunt down his family and get permission to tell a cute funny story about their dead son.

Charles died of AIDS in the late eighties. I'm sure many of those anonymous people I spent the evening with are also dead. See? It's not a good backdrop for a sweet little story. We all have lost many wonderful, loving, talented people to AIDS. We all know the heartbreak. Please don't confuse the lighthearted moments of this story as a lack of grief. I still grieve for friends I've lost to AIDS, but you have my word that Charles would laugh his well-fucked ass off at my putting this story in a book.

From 1979 to 1981 Teller and I were doing a three-man show called *The Asparagus Valley Cultural Society* at the Phoenix Theatre on Broadway in San Francisco. The third member was a guy named Wier Chrisemer. He played xylophone and pipe organ, did funny monologues, and believed in god. He finally got his fill of working with a couple of heathens, but we did 965 shows together in that theater in North Beach. We were down the street from the Condor Club, where Carol Doda, the most famous topless dancer in the sixties, was still shaking her beautiful early aftermarket "twin 44s." We were across the street from the Mabuhay Gardens, where Teller and I would see the Dead Kennedys, Flipper, Black Flag, and a great band called Eye Protection.

The audience at the Phoenix Theatre outnumbered the performers by only 140. There wasn't a very large staff—a couple box office people, a manager, and Charles, the bartender. It was San Francisco and it was theater, so most everyone working with us was gay. Three years is a long time for a little theater show, and we all got to know each other pretty well. There was no stage door to the theater, and I'd walk in the front and greet Charles every night. If I was early enough, we'd chat for a while as he was preparing the bar for preshow.

Charles was just talking:* "You know, Penn, you don't know how hard it is to be a gay man living in a straight world."

"What the fuck are you talking about? This is San Francisco. I'm a straight man living in a fucking gay world."

"No, seriously, you don't have to go to restaurants and see two gay men making out, but I have to see breeders making out all the time."

"And that bothers you? Really?"

"How would you feel if men were making out all around you when you went out to dinner?"

"I'd feel fucking great. Why would that bother me? Men do make out on Castro and that doesn't bother me at all. Not one bit. I'm telling you, really, I wouldn't mind men fucking each other in the ass while I had dinner. I like people having sex."

"No, you wouldn't be comfortable. You just wouldn't. I don't see you hanging out at Club Baths."

"I would. Sure I would. I mean . . . sure. Fuck, I'd love to go. When are you going next? I'll go with you."

"You can't go to Club Baths."

"Why not?" This might be a civil rights issue.

"Straight guys don't go."

"How will they know I'm straight?"

Charles laughed. He laughed a lot. He kept laughing.

I didn't really know what he meant. Even after my night at the Club Baths, even after all these years, I still don't really know what he meant. He certainly demonstrated what he meant, but I still don't understand it. Was I born this way? Conditioned this way? Did I make a choice? I don't know. But Charles had thrown down the nicely decorated,

* I'm making up and improving all the dialogue in this story—it was thirty years ago, give a fellow a break.

fabulous gauntlet. Now I had something to prove. "They can't stop me from going. How will they know I'm straight?"

Charles laughed. "You're not going to go to Club Baths with me."

"Sure I am."

"You have to be a member."

"Bullshit. I mean, the initiation can't be much different from what people go there for anyway, right? I'll become a member."

"The membership is to make it a private club to get around certain laws. You know, people have sex right there, right in the club. Dirty nasty gay sex."

"I've heard about Club Baths. I know y'all go, and I've always wondered about it. I want to go."

"It's really hard-core. A breeder like you couldn't handle it."

"Fuck you."

"Really, you have to pay a membership fee."

"It can't be too much, right?"

"It's like sixty bucks."

"I'll pay."

"And you have to give your name. You'll be in some government databases."

"Hey, if they're coming for you, they can come for me. I'm King fucking Christian the Tenth of Denmark." (There wasn't Snopes.com back then; I didn't know that the story of the king of Denmark wearing a yellow Star of David on his arm to defy the Nazis was jive.) I asked him again when he was going to the club.

"I'll probably go this Sunday night."

"Fuck it, I'm going with you!"

"Yeah, sure."

That night, I did the show and then went home to my girlfriend Tracy. She had moved from back east to San Fran with me. She was a hot little bucket of fuck—way smart and way cool. I told her I was going to Club Baths with Charles. She posed the obvious question: "Is this your way of telling me something? Are you gay? You can't be gay. You're not gay. You love tits too much."

"Many gay men love tits. And everyone in the world loves your perfect tits, but no, I don't think I'm gay. I never thought about it much, but I've always wondered about Club Baths. I've heard about it, I've read about it. I want to see it. I want to experience it. And I want to prove to Charles that I'm not a fucking pussy."

"Getting fucked by a guy doesn't prove you're not a pussy."

"It sure does. Oh, it certainly does. In a court of fucking law."

"So, are you going to fuck? Are you going to blow a guy? Are you going to get blown? What do I do while you're gone? I can't go."

"Sit home and watch TV, I guess. Or go out with your friends. I don't know. Go blow a guy."

"Are you going to?"

"I don't know. I've never gotten turned on by a guy before, but this is supposed to be amazing sex. Really hard-core. These are people who know what they're doing, this is real fucking sex. If my cock gets hard there, I'll fuck something."

"That's the plan?"

"I guess. I don't know. I have no idea what will happen."

"You are so not fucking gay. You are so far from gay. You're going to be a straight guy walking around Club Baths."

"What the fuck does that mean?"

"You'll walk around Club Baths like a fucking farmer."

"There are gay farmers."

You notice I didn't deny I was going to walk around like a farmer. There was no denying that. I walk like a cartoon farmer. I lumber. I have an awful walk. You can hear me walk. I have horrible flat feet and I'm so fucking big that you can hear me dragging my ass from a mile away.

After Teller and I were on the Emmys the first time, my dad said, "They give you that wonderful introduction. They say nice things about you. There's a big band playing. The camera sees you looking great in your fancy tuxedo, and then you walk out like a farmer."

Of course there are gay farmers, but there aren't gay farmers who walk like me.

I made it clear I was going with Charles to Club Baths. It turns out

Tracy knew a lot about being gay. After we split up several months later (totally unrelated to my gay adventure), she started dating nothing but women. She has lived happily ever after as a lesbian. (Although I don't think any of her girlfriends ever walked like farmers.)

Anyway, there were still a few days to wait and I was bragging to everyone that I was going to Club Baths. I was going to be Charles's date. It was going to be great. I was nervous. I was excited.

I told my good friend Bernard that I was going. He felt competitive.

"I wouldn't be bothered by going," he said.

"You would too. You're a nice breeding homophobe."

"I am not."

"You are too. You talk a good fight, but you'd be just a scared little pussy if leather daddies with those hats were fucking all around you."

"Would not."

"Would too."

"I'm going with you."

"No you're not, I'm going with Charles. He's my date. You can go out with Tracy that night. Go hang with her and your girlfriend. The three of you can go to a movie or something; I'll be out watching guys fuck."

"I know Charles too. I'm going to ask him if I can go. I don't need your permission."

I decided that I'd better ask Charles first. He was a little insulted.

"I'm not running a field trip to the faggot zoo. This is a bad idea. Fuck you. We're not going."

Charles and I talked for a while longer and finally decided that Bernard could come with me. He would make it better. Charles wouldn't feel like he had to babysit the breeders. He would leave us, go off and get fucked, and we could keep each other company. It is pretty stupid to go to Club Baths with a straight guy as your date. This was the best plan. Charles would lead Bernard and me to the edge of dick-munchin' land and we'd be on our own.

As the day approached, Bernard and I talked to our girlfriends. We talked about it all the time. We wanted to be ready for anything. I told Bernard, "We don't want to be cockteasers, right? These are guys who are there to fuck. By walking in the door, we're saying we want to fuck. We don't want to give anyone the wrong idea. We don't want to lead anyone on. That's a douchebag thing to do for any sexual orientation. I've told Tracy that if my cock gets hard, I'll fuck something." I was still trying to one-up Bernard. I wanted to be the coolest. Even if my farmer DNA wouldn't allow me to walk the walk, I was going to talk the talk, and, if the vibe was right, fuck the fuck. Bernard kept right up with me. He said that if he got hard, he'd fuck too. We were both ready to prove it all night long.

Sunday finally arrived. It was time to go. It didn't matter what we wore; we'd be stripping to go in anyway. It didn't really matter what our hair looked like; we'd be in baths, right? Steam rooms and shit. Nothing mattered. This was all men. The cockteaser issue bothered us a bit. We didn't want to lead anyone on, so Bernard and I would be a couple. We would stay close together. We would hold hands. Our gay brothers would figure we already had our hookups, and so we wouldn't lead anyone on. It was a perfect plan.

Tracy thought it was stupid. "So, you gay losers are going to hold hands?"

"Well, you know, to signal that we're together."

"Why don't the two of you stay here and fuck each other and save a hundred and twenty bucks?"

"I guess I didn't mean we were going to hold hands."

"I'm sorry, what does 'we're going to hold hands' really mean? Is that gay code? What color handkerchief goes in what pocket to signal you like to hold hands?"

"You know, I mean, we'll be a couple, so we're not sending off the wrong signals."

"That's so nice of you to let the whole gay world down gently. You two are complete out-of-the-closet assholes."

Charles, Bernard, and I arrived at Club Baths, one very attractive, fit, confident, sexy, young gay man and two dipshits. I don't remember much about the building. I'm sure the web has all the details of the building and every room and what it was like back then, but I want to do this from memory. I remember we went right into the locker room. Charles stripped naked, grabbed his towel, folded his clothes, and locked his valuables up, and that's the last we saw of him until we left five hours later. Bernard and I stripped naked, put our clothes in clumps in our lockers, and struggled with our towels. It seemed that the men used one towel each and chose its placement carefully. If they had a great chest, they tied it around their waist; if they had a great ass, they just put it around their neck. It was a very easy decision for me—the towel didn't fit around my waist, so I had to represent a great cock and ass. Bernard tied his around his waist.

Bernard and I gave each other big smiles, held hands, and walked together into Grand gay fucking Central station. I was trying not to walk like a farmer, but I don't have a choice. It's nature and nurture. We looked around. It was a bathhouse. There were baths. I remember a really nice steam room and a Jacuzzi when we first went in. It was all very *Logan's Run,* if Farrah had a faucet. There's this comfortable hateful cliché that anonymous sex is sad and lonely because no one is smiling or laughing. Very few of the men were smiling and laughing, but it didn't seem sad and lonely, it seemed intense. There's a difference. They weren't there to flirt, they were there to fuck. All your *Playboy* foldouts will talk about laughing in bed, and funny men, and how important a sense of humor is in a man. I've enjoyed giggling before, during, and after sex. But there are other kinds of great sex that don't involve any laughing. There are kinds of sex that are focused and intense, and make you not feel like making little jokes. There is sex where the sex itself is all that matters. Playful, fun sex is great, but serious fucking is good too. Club Baths was nothing but serious-fucking fucking. They were more than cruising, they were prowling. There were some intense fuckers in Club Baths that night. Everyone knew why everyone who was at Club Baths was at Club Baths.

Bernard and I didn't have any idea at all why we were at Club Baths. We sat in the steam room, held hands, and told jokes. We giggled together. Bernard jumped into the Jacuzzi and splashed and we laughed.

We were the only ones who were laughing. We were the only ones holding hands. It'd be easy to spin this as we were the ones enjoying life, the ones full of joy, but that would be wrong. We were the ones who weren't going to have any real honest fun that night.

Charles was upstairs on the floor that had little individual rooms where couples or trios of men would go in to fuck and be fucked. I think you could also go out on the rooftop if you wanted to blow a guy in the warm San Francisco night. Bernard and I walked up and looked around, but we were more comfortable in the steam and bath rooms; we liked the bigger rooms better. There was a very dark little theater downstairs running gay porno. There was a weight room, where people could act out YMCA fantasies. There was a little snack cart with apple juice and muffins.

Bernard and I held hands and walked from room to room. Keep in mind that I'm huge, and Bernard is average size and thin. We both had unfashionable haircuts. We were both wet from playing in the Jacuzzi and one of us was walking like a naked farmer with a towel around his neck. We were there a long time. We went into the weight room and actually used the weight machines. We didn't bend over the bench press rack to get fucked. We tried to lift a little weight. We'd never lifted weights before, we were just playing. On the floor we were on, a few people were fucking in the corners, but there wasn't real sex out in the well-lit open. We didn't really watch anyone fuck; they were kind of around us, but no one was displaying it. I'm sure other nights that happened, but this wasn't a crowded night. This was Bring Your Sexually Remedial Breeder Coworker to the Club Day.

We went into the little movie theater and watched the gay porn for a long while. We were the only ones watching. There were couples all around us fucking, sucking, and jacking. We had only the reflected light from the screen so we couldn't see much, but gay sex was happening all around us. We certainly saw more sex than a gay guy would see from a straight couple at a downtown McDonald's. It sure didn't bother me. I would have proved my point to Charles, except Charles was a couple floors above us getting the living shit fucked out of him. There wasn't much gloating for me to do, so I nonchalantly squinted at blow jobs in a gay theater. Bernard and I were no longer holding hands—we thought that whispering jokes quietly to each other in the little gay movie theater was enough of a hint that we were spoken for.

We'd been there a few hours and not only had my cock not gotten hard, but we were bored. Really bored. We had promised to leave with Charles, and time may fly when you're getting reamed, but it drags on and on when you're walking like a farmer, drinking little bottles of apple juice, and holding hands with a straight guy from Jersey.

It was time to address the very well-hung and well-groomed elephant in the bathhouse. We didn't have to be holding hands. In the hours we'd been there, we had not teased one fucking cock. We hadn't gotten our asses grabbed, no one had bent over and offered us a man pussy, no one had asked us if we came there often or lived with our folks. No one had said a fucking word to us. No one had made eye contact with us. These guys are horny animals. They will fuck anything!

Go to the web, and you'll find gay sites for fatties, hairy guys, hung guys, small-dick guys (those sites don't jump to the top of Google but they must be there), sissy guys, butch guys, leather daddies, drag queens, twinks, bears—the list goes on and on. There's someone getting hard for everyone. And this was 1981; no one really knew enough about AIDS to be scared and careful. This was a fucking gay bathhouse! There was no stigma to being gay. There was no gay-bashing in there. No one would ever be called "faggot" without irony or some sort of BDSM turn-on humiliation scene. If one single patron had had the slightest desire for us, there was no downside to letting us know. There was no reason to be discreet. These were guys who desired anything. Listen to any preacher talk about San Francisco gays. The word "discerning" isn't used a lot. These fuckers weren't known for being picky.

I was a little hurt at the rejection, so . . . I started cruising. I let go of Bernard's hand and tried to make my feet less ducklike. I tried to not walk like a farmer. I tried to tighten up my little ass. I sucked in my stomach, I fluffed up my cock. Goddamn it to fucking hell, these guys would fuck anything, and I may not have been Wham!'s George Michael, but I was a subset of "anything," right? I left Bernard alone and I walked up and down. I made eye contact with every guy in the place. I tried smiling, I tried looking intense. I tried winking. I brushed up against other men. I worked it, girlfriend. I did that for about an hour.

Nothing.

I went back to holding hands with Bernard. At least when I was holding hands with Bernard the gay world had an excuse for not wanting to fuck me. If gay marriage had been legal then, I would have married Bernard and promised to be exclusive. Anything to not face the truth of universal rejection.

After about five hours of fighting off and disappointing not one single solitary gay soul, Charles finally came back downstairs. He had been fucked. Wow, had he been fucked. He had been used up. Every guy who hadn't wanted us had had Charles. He had been rode hard and put up wet.

"How did you do?" he asked, like it was a fishing trip.

I started to tell him about our evening. He cared as much about my take on the Club Baths as the other gay men had cared about my hot little fuck holes and swinging dick. Completely sated and satisfied, Charles got dressed quickly. He had been through a lot of towels that night. Mine was still around my neck. You'd have felt safe sending a three-year-old to bed with my towel. It hadn't seen any action at all. Bernard and I got dressed. We had gotten a lot of steam and hot water, and the cold early, early morning air of San Francisco felt great.

Charles lived close by, but it was a couple miles back to where I lived, and Bernard and I decided to walk. We needed to talk. The two of us had held hands and talked at the club, but it was time to really talk about the experience. It didn't take long for me to say to Bernard, "You know the expression 'You couldn't get laid in a women's prison with a fistful of pardons'? Well, we couldn't get eye contact at Club Baths."

"Fucking no one wanted us. Not at all." Bernard and I were really rejected and hurt.

"Yeah, asshole, straight guys are always saying, 'Man, if a fag ever came on to me, I'd punch him out.' Well, if they aren't a lot better looking than us, it's never going to happen. Or maybe it's just us."

"Did they know we were straight?"

"Did we just not give off the gay vibe?"

I don't know. I still don't know. I've told this story to a bunch of friends—gay and straight—and they just laugh in my face. I guess I'm that butt-ugly, or there's a straight smell or something.

As we walked through the San Francisco night, we were completely perplexed and very hungry. We decided to stop at Clown Alley for some burgers.

"Straight guys do not go to Club Baths," I said. "Who would? No one would. I mean, guys with wives and children, guys who say they're straight go to Club Baths. Guys who are lying to themselves about being straight. I thought we might be lying to ourselves about being straight. I mean, if you saw this in a book, you wouldn't believe it. You wouldn't believe the big asshole just wanted to make a point. You wouldn't believe he just wanted to see what it was like. No way; you'd know that he really just wanted to get fucked. He was a closet case who couldn't admit it, so he pretended he was going for another reason. Like guys who go to strip clubs for the sociology, or look at stroke mags for the articles. No one could have thought we were straight. We were holding hands, for cocksucking Christ's sake, and then we weren't holding hands. We were available. I mean, fuck."

Bernard summed it up: "We are such losers, we couldn't pass for gay at Club Baths."

When we left Clown Alley with our burgers, we were tired and had gotten pretty silly. We were laughing our asses off about not being able to pass as gay. We were speculating on what gave us away. We talked about my walk and Bernard's nose. We talked about our bodies. Bernard got to *really* laughing. He got to choking-on-his-hamburger and close-to-puking laughing. He was dying. He was laughing so hard, he couldn't stand up. He put his arm around my shoulders and neck to steady himself. I was laughing so hard, I couldn't help much. I put my arms around him. We needed to hold each other up. Just then, a car full of young men pulled out of the Clown Alley parking lot, rolled down a window, threw a beer can at us, and yelled, "Faggots!"

"YMCA"

—The Village People

Scuba Fucking

I wanted to be published in *Reader's Digest* and *Penthouse* since I first jerked off to each of them (*Penthouse*, with all those letters, and *Reader's Digest*, with "I Am Jane's Breast" and "I Am Joe's Man-gland"). It would have been cool if *RD* and *PH* printed the same article, but that's too much to hope for. I didn't want them to hire me or do a Penn & Teller story (I think they both did that anyway). I wanted to do it for real. I wanted to submit something like a citizen. Some "Humor in Uniform" for *Reader's Digest* and some jack-off story for *Penthouse*. I've never been in uniform, but I have jacked off, so I sent something to *Penthouse*. I've told people that my letter got printed in *Penthouse*, but I don't think I've ever really seen it in print and I can't find it online; however, I found my letter on my computer. I remembered it having the line "I was in San Francisco working in a comedy/magic duo, I'll call it Penn & Teller," but as it turns out, that's not in there.

I wrote this (and did the fucking underwater) way back in the days before *Bullshit!,* so I still thought I had to be a little careful about image. Since I've had my cock out on *Penn & Teller: Bullshit!* and written about going to a gay bathhouse, this seems pretty tame, but it's still fun. I sure hope someone somewhere can masturbate to this. (If you can, let me know, because it would really be a dream come true. And if you're in uniform when you rub one out, maybe we can sell that to *Reader's Digest* together.) What follows is what I sent them.

And yes, it's a true story.

Dear Penthouse,

This is a true story. I wrote it up for some guys on my computer BBS and they suggested I send it to you. Now, I may have been born yesterday, but I stayed up all night. I'm aware that the letters in your magazine are not entirely written by real people but rather by you, the fake person reading this letter. But I didn't know that when I first started using Forum *to jerk off, and it's been a dream for some time to write a* Penthouse *letter, so I figured I'd send it on. I know it's really long but this is the way it happened. If you want to use it, you edit it.*

I've asked Alex about using his name and he says fine, and he's a public figure in San Francisco, so I think it's way funny to say, "I'll call him Alex Bennett." I DO NOT want to use my name because it might confuse the little Penn & Teller image we have, but those who heard me on the air in SF will recognize the story anyway and get a good laugh.

If you can use it, great. If you can't, thanks again for all the great jerking off you've given me.

Every Inch of My Love,
Penn Jillette

Letter to *Penthouse Forum:*

PENN JILLETTE

Dear Penthouse,

I never thought I'd write a letter to Penthouse, but I finally had an experience that I think might interest your readers.

I was a guest on a morning talk/comedy radio show in San Francisco. The host of the show—I'll call him Alex Bennett—is a good friend, and I'm on the show often. We were discussing a vacation I was planning with a girlfriend to the Caribbean. We were planning a trip to a small island near the equator to do lots of scuba diving. Because discussions of scuba don't hold people's attention during "drive time," Alex asked if my date and I were going to be able to have sex underwater. I said, with a great deal of bravado, that it was a done deal, of course we would have sex underwater.

Alex asked me to put my money where my mouth was and bet me, on the air, $100 that I could not have an orgasm under forty feet of seawater. He had thrown down the gauntlet, and I took the bet. When he found out that my "dive buddy" was to be a model he had seen on TV, he began to worry, but in the end felt secure that the pressure (of winning the bet, rather than the pressure of forty feet of water) would stop me from spurting in Davy Jones's locker.

I am not a very experienced diver, but I have access to some real pros who were more than happy to give me advice. They assured me that Alex had taken a "sucker bet." I would win. The only problem, they said, was keeping the pussy moist enough to fuck. The salt of the sea "dries up" the mucous membranes and it can be a really gritty fuck if you don't plan ahead. The divers I talked to had experimented with many lubricants (one even claimed to have done it with the silicone used for ship motor lubrication) and they concluded that coconut oil was the way to go. Their other piece of advice was to apply the oil on shore, topside. "Get her wet on the inside before she's wet on the outside" seemed to be the aphorism.

I planned all this with my "dive buddy," and she felt confident that the $100 was as good as in the bank. She has a professional model™–

quality body and face. She's five feet ten with firm medium-size tits, a perfect ass, and a face that, alone, can get anyone's dick hard. This woman can make a dead man cum. She was ready.

We arrived on the island and took a few dives to get into the swim of it. It was the best diving I've ever seen, and because the hotel is just for divers, air tanks were always available and anyone was welcome to dive the reef off the wharf at any time.

When the day arrived, we decided I would wear boxer shorts and she would wear a tiny string bikini. My dick would come right out the fly, and the fabric of her bathing suit would only have to slide to one side to make her completely accessible. We started preparing in our room. She sucked my cock for a while, greased my hard cock up with coconut oil, and carefully put my cock back in my boxers. I ate her cunt, and even though the coconut oil seemed redundant in her dripping pussy, I applied it liberally with my fingers. We were pretty greasy.

We went down to the dock and got all our equipment. Scuba is a very proppy sport, and it was hard to do all the buckles and read all the gauges when we still felt in the middle of fucking and a little glazed. It was a bit scary. We swam out to the side of the reef, went down until our depth gauges read about fifty feet, and found a place to stand. We were told by other divers that it was much cooler if you were just floating, but we wanted to get our bearings to start. She had undone her top while swimming down and as she stood on the reef with the vest straps flanking her naked tits, she was ready.

I took the regulator out of my mouth, held my breath, and sucked on her tits. She has big nipples anyway, and the cold of the water and the blue tint of the filtered light made them look amazing. I sucked on her nipple hard until I needed air, took a breath off the regulator, and went back to sucking. After repeating that process a few times on each breast, I pulled her bikini bottom aside, licked her clit, and exhaled, tickling her cunt with the air bubbles. She pulled my head up; we both took our regulators out and kissed really hard and salty. She climbed down my body and pulled my dick out of my boxers. The magnification of the water does wonders for one's ego, and the blue tint of the water gave my hard-on a really pleasant purple hue. She did a remarkable job of breath control, sucking my cock between breaths and blowing air bubbles against my balls.

During all this we went away from the reef to be "weightless." It was really difficult to keep the buoyancy and depth constant with the two of us, with no reference points and our minds wandering away from gauges and toward fucking. There were lots of fish around, and I was keeping an eye on my dick (this is not a joke, yellowtails are used to being fed underwater and they will bite).

She likes sex fairly rough, so I took my regulator out of my mouth again and bit her nipple hard. I heard her scream with pleasure through her regulator, and this may have been the best part of the whole experience. We were really excited at this point, breathing hard and going through our air like crazy.

It was time to fuck. I don't think we needed the oil, my cock went in easy, and the "weightlessness" was really trippy. This woman always enjoys sex, and as we fucked underwater she completely forgot where she was and began screaming, sending us up and down, which scared me a little (it's very dangerous to change pressure too fast, you can get little bubbles in your brain that kill you). We fucked really hard; I was able to spin us around and upside down and get my finger up in her asshole. She came a couple of times, and even through the water I heard her screaming out of the regulator. It was really an out-of-the-world fuck.

Now (here's the important part for the bet), while I had my dick in her cunt I felt that kind of half-cum thing (where you feel an orgasm and you want to take a little break but you know you're going to cum again in a little while and really spurt) inside her. My dick was jumping around in her cunt and I was making those white-boy-James-Brown sounds and stuff. After that I pulled out of her, grabbed my dick, and started jerking off while she played with my balls.

We'd been there a while and ALL these fish were around (yellowtails, parrot, and trumpet fish—I don't think they were watching us, I think they thought this might be our way of getting food for them), and we had gone from forty feet to seventy feet and back again a couple times. She took her regulator out of her mouth and tried to make me cum in her mouth, but I knew that timing was going to be way too complicated. I jerked for a while, looking at fish and her hard cold nipples, and then I looked at my air supply. We'd only been down eighteen minutes, but I was way below 1,500 pounds. That means I was using air more than twice as fast as normal.

We headed back, skipping our decompression "safety stop" (which we could have really needed), and went back home. My "dive buddy" was freezing from diving without her wet suit. When we got into bed we fucked for a long time and I came hard. When we finished this shore fuck session, she was elated because we had won the bet and I was bummed because we'd lost. She said she felt me cum inside her. I said that I felt that Alex wanted a spurt, he wanted a "money shot." Now, on this trip we were averaging three fucking sessions a day, and even though we always had fun, sometimes I just didn't "have that much jam." It would feel like I was cumming but nothing would squirt out. This is what had happened underwater.

We tried one more underwater fuck, but right after I put it in we started floating up—I'd hit the wrong button on my buoyancy control vest and we went up almost twenty feet fast. This is very dangerous and it freaked us enough that that was the end of that session. These were the only two fuck sessions that we planned. We couldn't do it spontaneously, because my "buddy" really needed a wet suit to dive without freezing and we couldn't fuck with her in a wet suit. Also, she might have been wet enough without the oil, but we weren't sure and she wasn't comfortable greasing up in front of the other divers on the boat.

I really didn't know if I won or lost. I felt Alex wanted a "money shot" underwater, with fish gobbling up my sperm like so many yellow-tailed biker chicks, but maybe just orgasm was fine. I'm sure I could have given a good spurt if we laid off sex for twenty-four hours beforehand, but fuck that shit, it was only a hundred bucks and some pride, for Christ's sake. I talked to Alex, and we decided we would call it a tie. I didn't make a penny, and I didn't pay anything. But all things considered, I won.

Plan the dive
Dive the plan,
(Name and address withheld by request)

"Divers Do It Deeper"

—David Allan Coe

The Bible's Fifth Commandment

**Honor thy father and thy mother,
that thy days may be long upon the land which
the lord thy god has given thee.**

I have a very good friend who read this one and said that it really has to depend on who your family is. I guess, if I want to be logical, I have to accept that that's true. But it breaks my heart.

ONE ATHEIST'S FIFTH SUGGESTION

Be there for your family. Love your parents, your partner, and your children. (Love is deeper than honor, and parents matter, but so do spouse and children.)

Sister

I was at the Terrorist Starbucks with Sister and a bunch of my goofball friends. It's the Terrorist Starbucks because they say the 9/11 religious people planned part of their murders at this Vegas Buckys. If you went there for coffee in the first few years after the Twin Towers attack, some of the baristas would claim to have watched them plotting for god. I don't believe the killers were really ever there. After that much evil hits, our memories all get a little fucked. But I still call it the Terrorist Starbucks.

I didn't leave out the word "my" before "Sister." That was what I always called her. Her name was Valda, the same as my mom's name, but calling her by her first name would have seemed disrespectful. My sister was twenty-three years old when I was born and married when I was three years old. I was her ring bearer and I was cute as a button, motherfucker; I've seen the pictures.

Sister and I were full siblings and have no other brothers or sisters. No one between us. I suppose it's possible that our parents planned to have two children twenty-three years apart, but it seems more likely that I was a mistake. They might have used the word "surprise," but I never talked to my parents or Sister about sex. They weren't the kind of people who talk about sex. I am the kind of person who talks about sex a lot. I'm hoping that I can get through this tearful writing about Sister without writing about my cock.

Reading about Jack Nicholson and Bobby Darin each finding out, as adults, that their sisters were actually their moms, I was kind of ready for that surprise. I was so close to my mom, but I guess I could have been that close to her as my grandmother. However, there was no deathbed confession from Mom and no deathbed confession from Sister, so I guess I'm not destined for anything as great as *Chinatown* or that psycho translation of "Mack the Knife." There were people in my hometown who had been in the hospital with Mom when I was born, so if they were lying about it, they sure did a good job.

I had Mom and Dad in my life for half of their lives. I was born when Mom was forty-five, and Mom and Dad both died at around ninety. I was fifty when my daughter was born. Having older parents is great, except for that dying thing. Sister being older was wonderful, but she recently died too. She got to watch me on *Dancing with the Stars* with her friends at her very nice nursing home, and she got to meet my children before she died. Going on *Dancing with the Stars* sure is goofy. It can knock out of one's head any illusions one has about being in the "arts," but if you have elderly people you love, it'll make them very happy and popular with their friends.

Sister died a little young of old age, and when she died, there went the only person I was in contact with who knew me as a child. There was no longer anyone to call every day and talk about what my toddlers, Mox and Zz, had done that day and compare it to me when I was a child. When my mom and dad died, it seemed impossible that I could miss anyone more. When Sister died, I missed her more.

People used to say that Sister and I were opposites. She was so quiet and polite. I'm not quiet. She was sweet. I'm not. Everyone liked her. There wasn't a Facebook page dedicated to calling her a cunt, like there is for her brother. Being a tour guide at Historic Old Deerfield, taking three people at a time through the collection of two-hundred-year-old crafts, was as showbizzy as she ever got. Her brother was on *Dancing with the Stars* and knows Wayne Newton.

Because of all our fucked-up generations, I guess you could say she assumed the role of grandparent for me. She would take me on Sundays when Mom and Dad went to numismatic shindigs. Sister would care for me and give me all the candy I wanted. She had her own children, so Mox and Zz's first cousins are now knocking on fifty years old.

If you want to raise a monster like me, just fill your children with unconditional love. Not just California heart-on-the-sleeve-hug love (when Mom was on her deathbed, I told her I loved her. She said, "Well, of course you do, you always do, why did you think you had to say something like that?" Saying I loved Mom and Dad was like saying I was breathing; it really didn't have to be mentioned. We didn't hug much, but our hugs were not like hugging my agents in L.A.), but real love. And while you're at it, throw in pure unconditional love from a sibling. That will give you a person who is twelve feet tall and bulletproof.

Back to the Terrorist Buckys. The conversation turned from the 9/11 terrorists to the Unabomber. Everyone took turns commiserating with the brother of the Unabomber turning in his dangerous and mentally ill brother. Each one of the show folk at the table talked about how hard it would be to make that decision.

Sister didn't get it. She was sincerely puzzled. She was often left out of our conversations—we talked about music she hadn't heard or movies she hadn't seen—and she'd sit politely as we rudely left her out.

I still hadn't said anything myself about the Unabomber's brother. I was watching Sister. She was really confused and showing it. Sister knew about what was going on in the world; it was hard to believe she didn't know about the Unabomber being turned in by his brother.

"Sister, you know the Unabomber, right—the environmental guy who killed and wounded those scientists? His brother turned him in."

"Yes, I know. I just don't know what's hard."

"They're talking about how hard it would be for his brother to turn him in to the Feds. The brother figured out his brother was the Unabomber. His brother turned him in; that must have been hard."

"Yes, I know about the Unabomber and his brother, but I don't see what's hard about it."

Everyone got ready for Sister to explain that if someone was killing people, you had to stop them. She was such a gentle person. She had raised money for the police of Greenfield, Massachusetts, to buy bulletproof vests.

Nope. That's not what she meant.

"I would never turn in a member of my family. Never. Not to anyone for any reason. I would never turn against Penn. Never."

Sister was never confrontational. She didn't say crazy shit like her brother does. My friends were shocked. She left no room for debate, but my dirtball friends elbowed in some room for debate. They came up with a few variations on the Jack Bauer torture argument: "Penn has put an atomic bomb in the center of Manhattan. It will kill everyone, millions of people. If you turn him in, they can stop it from going off, and it'll save millions of people. You'd turn him in then, right?"

It was like they had said to her, "You can flap your arms and fly under your own power, right? And then you can eat a twelve-pound bowling ball in one bite, right?"

"No, never. I would never turn in my brother. I'm on his side no matter what. There's nothing he can do to change that. Nothing."

I had never seen Sister push this hard in a discussion. She always sat on the sidelines; now she was in the center. Now they were hypothetically off in outer space, with me blowing up the whole world, and it could all be stopped by her dropping a dime. I was no longer listening. I was just looking at Sister and thinking. Here was a seventy-three-year-old gray-haired New England woman dressed in her Sunday clothes to be out at a Starbucks with her brother's collection of musicians, comedians, and showgirls in jeans and tattoos, and she wasn't budging. She couldn't even understand that it was a question.

I can't imagine loving Sister more. I can't imagine it. And as much as I feel that white light/white heat diamond-bullet love for Sister, she loved me more. I might decide not to rat her out in these hypothetical games, but I would have to think about it. It wasn't just that she couldn't understand ratting me out; she couldn't understand having to think about ratting me out.

Shortly after that trip to Vegas, she started getting sick. She had a few little strokes and a lot of trouble walking. She got MRSA in the hospital. I saw her a bunch more and we visited her with her little niece and nephew wearing masks. We had lots more talks and I held her hand. I looked at her.

But when I think of love, I don't just think of her holding little Zz and singing songs Mom used to sing to us. I think of Sister not even understanding that there was a decision to be made in choosing me over the world.

I sure hope I learned something from Sister. I want Mox and Zz to feel that pure immoral love that Sister felt for me. If Moxie and Zolten Jillette make plans to set up nuclear devices all over the planet and I know about this plan and how the FBI can stop them . . . you better kiss your ass good-bye.

"Nuclear War"

—Sun Ra

Passing Down the Joy of Not Collecting Stamps

There was a book out a while ago about atheist parenting. I'm not going to tell you what it was called. They asked me to write an article for them. It was like no money, but I thought it was a good cause. I wrote the article and the editors told me it was the only article they wanted to change for content. They thought I was too negative toward religion, and they thought the word "fuck" would turn people off. I tried to explain that sometimes the word "fuck" turns people on. Who cares? I let them water down what I said, but I promised to never mention the book by name anywhere. If you still want to read it, go fuck yourself. Why would anyone want a book on atheist parenting that teaches atheist parents to be half-assed about their beliefs? I liked what I wrote, and now I have my own book, so I'll go through the original article and make it even more negative toward religion, and I'll write "fuck" in various forms.

Saint Ignatius Loyola, the founder of the Jesuit order, wrote, "Give me the child until he is seven and I will show you the man." Some web pages say that might really be Francis Xavier's quotation. Others say it was "some Jesuit" who said it, and all the careful scholarly web pages credit it to "some guy."

Little children have to trust adults or they die. Trust has to be built in. So while you're teaching them to eat, stay out of traffic, and not drink too much of what's underneath the sink, you can abuse that trust and burn in the evil idea that faith is good. It'll often stick with them longer than not drinking bleach. It seems if someone snuck the idea of faith into you at an early age, you're more likely to do it to your own children.

If your childhood trust was not abused with faith or if somehow you kicked it in your travels down the road, your work is done. You don't have to worry too much about your children. You don't ever have to teach atheism. You don't have to teach an absence of guilt for things they didn't do. As atheist parents, you just have one more good reason to keep your children away from priests. Tell your children the truth as you see it and let the marketplace of ideas work as they grow up. An "anonymous reader" of James Randi's Swift web page wrote, "Atheism is a religion like not collecting stamps is a hobby." Maybe it was Francis Xavier.

You have to work hard to get children to believe nonsense (outside of their make-believe sessions). If you're not desperately selling lies, the work is a lot easier. My children are still in preschool, but even when they were babies we were still a little bit careful of what we said. When someone sneezes we say "That's funny," because it is. We don't have any friends who are Christards or into any kind of faith-based hooey, so our children will just think that "damn it" naturally follows "god" like "fucker" naturally follows "mother."

That's cool. That's easy.

It's an unfashionable belief in the atheist community, but truth just needs to be stated; it doesn't have to be hyped. I know, I do a lot of hyping of atheism, but remember what Bob Dobbs said: "I don't practice what I preach because I'm not the kind of person I'm preaching to."

There is no god, and that's the simple truth. If every trace of any single religion were wiped out and nothing were passed on, it would never be created exactly that way again. There might be some other nonsense in its place, but not that exact nonsense. If all of science were wiped out, it would still be true and someone would find a way to figure it all out again.

Without hype, Lot's salt-heap ho would never be thought of again. Without science, Earth still goes around the sun, and someday someone would find a way to discover that again. Science is so important because it's a way to find truth, but the truth doesn't depend on it. Reality exists outside of humans. Religion does not. The bad guys have to try to get the children early to keep their jive alive. We good guys should try to get the truth out there, but the stakes just aren't as high for us. Most anyone who is serious about science will lose some faith. Maybe not all their faith, but they'll lose a hunk of it before getting that Nobel Prize. No matter how bad the polls on the general population of Americans look, the people who do science for a living aren't being fooled. Evolution is the truth. And with truth comes a lack of panic. I don't lose sleep over creation myths being taught in public schools. Who trusts anything from government schools? Does anyone besides me really believe that marijuana is a gateway drug? "Better to be uneducated than educated by your government," as either I or Thomas Jefferson said. The bad guys always have to fight for their ideas to be taught. They must cheat. Government force, propaganda, and hype are the tools you desperately need when you're wrong. Truth abides.

Doctor Richard Dawkins had a Christian education, but he kicked that way before taking his seat in the Darwin Barcalounger at Oxford. The bad guys got the Dawk until he was seven. So what? That race has been run; they fought the truth and the truth won. I went to Sunday school and the reality of the creationist myth stayed as true for me as the certainty that the Greenfield High School football team was going to win the Turkey Day game because we had P . . . E . . . P. . . PEP! PEP! PEP! Jesus Christ, doesn't anyone but Paul Simon and me remember it was all crap we learned in high school anyway and we children always knew it?

Evolution was true before Darwin. Evolution was true in the sixteenth century when Loyola did or didn't write that quotation. Evolution has been true as long as there has been life on earth, and it always will be true. If there is life on other planets, it'll be true there too. If you pick your side carefully, you don't have to fight as hard.

All this assumes you're an out-of-the-closet atheist parent. Truth doesn't live in the closet. You have to make it clear to everyone, including your children, that there is no god. If you're not doing that every chance you get, then the other side will win. They'll win only in the short term; but we only get to live in the short term. You don't have to fight, but you have to do your part—you have to tell the truth. You have to be honest. You don't have to force schools to say there's no god, but you have to say it yourself. You have to say it all the time. No one can relax in a closet.

Those of us who are out-of-the-closet atheist parents have all that extra time on Sunday mornings to love our children. We can use that time to hold them, laugh, and dance around together. Tell your children there's no god and be done with it. Jesus Christ, your children aren't stupid.

"I Fought the Law"

—Sonny Curtis and The Crickets

"I Fought the Law"

—The Bobby Fuller Four

"I Fought the Law"

—The Clash

Up Your Santa Claus Lane

The most important thing in the world is to tell our children the truth, but we lie to them all the time. By "we," I don't mean people in general, and by "our children," I don't mean children in general. I mean my wife and I lie to our daughter, Moxie, and our son, Zolten, right to their beautiful little smiling faces. We tell our loving little children, who must trust us with their very lives, that Disneyland is never open except when we're already planning on taking them there. We tell them the frozen yogurt place is closed after dinner on Wednesdays, and that's after we've lied that frozen yogurt is ice cream. The frozen yogurt place stretches the truth that frozen yogurt is even one wispy RCH healthier than ice cream. The frozen yogurt people may be stretching the truth, but we are lying sacks of shit to the people we care most about in our lives. It's not preplanned lying, it's lazy lying.

I feel weird about lying to my children every time I do it. I do it less than my wife, but only because I do less child wrangling than my wife. I try to tell them the real reason I want them to do or not do something, but the real reason is often "Because I said so."

Maybe it is better just to lie.

Emily and I don't lie to our children about Santa Claus.

Santa Claus is an atheist battleground. Some do, some don't. Michael Goudeau does, and he certainly has his atheist/skeptical cred. He's the real deal in the no-god camp. He's won a Writers Guild award and has been nominated for a zillion Emmys (another lie we tell: "It's an honor just to be nominated") for writing with us on *Penn & Teller: Bullshit!* He was the cohost on my radio show for a couple of years, and he's been my close friend forever. We agree on almost everything except sports (he likes them), his shitty musical taste (he has it), and Santa Claus (he lies about him). I know a lot of great dads and Goudeau is one of them.

Every Xmas time, Goudeau argues with my wife about Santa. I think the Goudeaus do the whole production—coming down the chimney, milk and cookies, reindeer, you name some winter seasonal bullshit and the Goudeaus do it. The Jillettes don't do any of it. Not really. This year my wife bent a little and we had a "The Jillettes Don't Celebrate Xmas Tree." It wasn't even a pine tree, and no angels. And not one piece of reindeer shit. I'm not sure I'm that against Santa Claus myself (it seems like a bit less of a lie than the yogurt thing), but, man, my wife sure has a hard-on for that jolly little elf.

In interviews, when I'm asked "How do you atheists celebrate Xmas?" I answer that the Jillette atheists don't do anything. The interviewer assumes that I'm the goofy Scrooge and I'm denying our children the joy of Xmas. I am denying our children the joy of Xmas, but I'm sure doing it with my wife's blessing, so to speak. It was her idea, but I'll take responsibility. I agree with her. I agree with her because she's right. I love Goudeau, but I don't sleep with him every night. Another friend of mine, a cynical socialist (isn't that redundant?), insisted that his daughter be force-fed Santa, so when the disillusionment hit her hard, she'd crash and throw out the baby Jesus with the Santa bathwater. This is the same guy who wanted to send his daughter to Catholic school to be sure she'd be a hard-core atheist her whole life. Socialists love that manipulation shit. It's good that he couldn't convince his wife to go along with him.

I love tradition and I love ritual. My mom and dad's Jillette household celebrated Xmas with all the trimmings. We had a tree with those bubbling lights that never really worked, and we strung colored popcorn. We had a crèche on top of the TV with real straw and a wax candle Santa standing in the nativity, a bit out of place at three times the size of the wise men, wearing arctic clothing and with a waxy wick sticking out of his red hat. Monster giant Santa stood laughing at the baby Jesus standing next to an out-of-scale giant Styrofoam Frosty the Snowman, who looked higher than Keith Richards in the basement at Nellcôte. Once you're buying virgin birth and dying for other people's sins, a talking snowman and a fat elf in a flying sleigh is easy.

I've had a bone to pick with Frosty since I was a child. I begin ranting about Frosty incessantly from the first time Xmas music pops up on the radio until about Valentine's Day, when Sam Cooke's "Cupid" takes over my head. The song "Frosty the Snowman" makes me crazy: "There must have been some magic in that old silk hat they found, for when they placed it on his head, he began to dance around." Correlation is not causation, you stupid Gene Autry and the Cass County Boys song–composing motherfucker! It's this kind of sloppy thinking that is the real "reason for the season." Oh, and the other reindeer didn't all love Rudolph for any sort of humanitarian (reindeeratarian?) reason, they just needed him for his bioluminescent nose that one night—we know they will all go back to disrespecting him, laughing at him, shunning him, and calling him names the first moderately unfoggy Xmas Eve that rolls around.

My mom and dad lied to me about Santa. When I was very young, my dad was a jail guard and he had to work Xmas morning, so we had our celebration on Xmas Eve, and it was explained to me that Santa started his annual journey in New England, because we were so close to the North Pole. I bought it.

Many Xmas people think that only those with bitter childhood Xmas memories would deprive their children of Xmas, but I have only fond memories of Xmas with my mom and dad. Even when Mom and Dad's Xmas tree changed to plastic, then finally to a little ceramic one my mom made at a senior center crafts class to sit on top of the TV, I still loved Xmas with my mom and dad. I liked my mom's system of keeping the cards with the toys so I could write all my thank-yous. I liked the zillion Mounds bars that I vomited up one Xmas morning that put me off candy coconut to this day. I liked my mom and dad marveling at the shoebox-size brick of a first cell phone that Teller gave me one year. My mom and dad felt a joy in watching me open presents, a joy they said I would only understand once I had children. They were right, but I don't get that joy from my children on December 25, and we don't talk about Santa Claus. Our children hear about Santa Claus from their peers, but he's less of a big deal in that circle than Dora the Explorer. And since I tore Frosty a new snowy and coal asshole, allow me to bitch that "Dora" and "explorer" don't rhyme any more than "action" and "Jackson," unless you're a lobsterman in Maine. When the movie *Action Jackson* came out, Teller was suggesting slug lines: "*Action Jackson:* it's just assonance," and "*Action Jackson:* you tell him it doesn't rhyme." Unfortunately, Carl Weathers never consulted Teller.

"Let's take the Christ out of Xmas" would be a fine slogan for the Winter Solstice, and American advertising has done some wonderful work toward that goal. The right-wing fucking nut jobs are correct—Xmas is becoming secularized. That's a good thing. It's secular to the point that the Christ part of Xmas doesn't really piss the Jillettes off too much. I just wish that those who are secularizing Xmas (or taking it back from the Christians—it did start out as a pagan holiday) would admit they want it secular to sell more shit to more different people. When I was in high school I had a girlfriend, Linda.† She was way smart (still is) and way sexy (still is). My parents never talked to me about sex or drugs, but her parents talked about little else. They were liberals. They listened to Bob Dylan (maybe not literally, but in my memory they were playing *Blonde on Blonde* all the time) and had *The Joy of Sex* on their coffee table, probably in Spanish (I was too embarrassed to open it). They read novels in Spanish. They took a bus from Massachusetts to Washington, DC, to protest the Vietnam war. They were totally groovy liberals who I'm sure are now fine with all the killing overseas, because Obama is in charge

† Linda is not her real name—she no longer minds people knowing that we went to Cape Cod just to sleep together and fuck, but I don't want to be writing snotty stuff about her liberal parents. I saw them at the county fair last time I visited and I really liked them.

and he's liberal. In high school their daughter and I had an opportunity to go to Cape Cod and stay on a houseboat together. We were so excited because we'd get a chance to sleep together. Really sleep. We'd done every sex act known to Henry Miller, but we hadn't really slept together. We'd never heard each other snore. We were very excited. My parents were fine with my going to Cape Cod with Linda. If they hadn't been fine, we would have had to talk about sex, and my parents sure weren't going to do that. We were old-style New England. Her parents were okay with us going to Cape Cod, like they were liberally okay with us fucking, but made a comment that they knew we didn't care about Cape Cod (who does?), we were just going to stay on the houseboat so we could sleep together. Linda was so fucking insulted and angry. She was outraged. How could her parents say something like that? She wanted them to say we wanted to go to Cape Cod for . . . what? For the . . . cod? She was offended that they didn't believe we were going to Cape Cod as tourists and we would just happen to stay on a houseboat. She felt they should take us at our word. She thought they should act like they believed the lie.

Linda was just embarrassed about her parents talking about us sleeping together. She was embarrassed, but this is one of the things that bugs me so much about some liberals that I've known. I'm writing about liberals that I know personally. I'm not writing about liberals in general—I don't know liberals in general. The self-identified "progressives" and "liberals" that I know are bitter fucking manipulative hateful whack jobs. The self-identified "Tea Party" people I know are bitter fucking manipulative hateful whack jobs. The common denominator is not politics. The common denominator is me. The liberals I know will say that medical marijuana is a foot in the door, the first step to legalizing marijuana for everyone. And when the right wing accuses them of wanting that same exact thing, they ridicule the right-wingers and say "What about the people suffering horribly from cancer who need to toke?" My liberal friends think the literal reading of the Bible is nonsense and we should celebrate other religions and cultures, and when the right says "They're trying to take the Christ out of Christmas," liberals go bug-fucking-nutty. Just about everyone who writes and produces comedy on TV is a fucking lefty and is pushing the agenda of gay rights and liberal causes, and my liberal friends—even though they're against the fucking corporations running TV—are thrilled with those writers, but when the fucking psycho right wing says the TV writers are doing just what they're doing, my liberal friends scoff. I think that's why my lefty friends are so comfortable calling the Tea Party people racist, even though the Tea Party doesn't say they themselves are racist. My lefty friends just assume that everyone lies about their real agenda. Racism is evil collectivist bullshit, marijuana (and all drugs—fuck the FDA) should be legal, let's get the Christ out of Xmas, and Linda and I were going to Cape Cod to sleep together and have intense pre-AIDS, no-holes-barred teenage sex.

And Hollywood is lefty. So what? You can say what you want about *Penn & Teller: Bullshit!*, but we don't fucking lie about our agenda. We are libertarian atheists, and even though most of our shows aren't about that (as a matter of fact it would be hard to tell any of that from our live show in Vegas), if you do read some atheist libertarian vibe in something we do, it's probably because we put it there. Why wouldn't oversimplifying, heartless, childish libertarians put their crazy selfish ideas in their shows, just like the commie TV writers put their shit in their situation comedies?

Just fucking cop to it.

As much as I'd love Xmas to be a celebration of commercialism with no religious overtones, it's not quite all the way there yet. I'm sure it'll get there. Commercialism is beautiful and wonderful and open and real, and belief in Jesus is superficial and creepy zombie stuff. If the urban legend about Santa being created by Coca-Cola were true, I might be able to get behind it, but Santa still has too much baggage on his sleigh besides toys.

The Goudeaus lied to their children completely, but the Goudeau children worked together and finally figured out that there was no Santa Claus. Joey, the older brother, started it off with the tooth fairy. He busted his mom and said, "So you and Dad are the tooth fairy?" Theresa answered, "Yes, Joey," and Joey followed up with the logical conclusion: "So you and Dad fly all over the world taking children's teeth out from under their pillows and giving them money?" Yup, that was his thinking. He told his little sister, Emily Peach, and she went the other way with the logical conclusion, and after Joey and Emily talked for a while, the tooth fairy, Santa, and the Easter Bunny all bit the dust. It was Mom and Dad, and there was no flying-around-the-world involved at all.

Our children are four and five, and surprisingly Santa doesn't come up too much. It's kind of like god—selling the shit is hard; not selling the shit is easy. It just doesn't come up much. But we're trying to create our own traditions. I've already mentioned one of them: when someone sneezes, we don't say "God bless you." We weren't even comfortable with "Bless you." "*Gesundheit*" is really fun to say, but it's about "healthiness," and that's a little too Colbert for our family's taste. So we go with "That's funny." We say "That's funny" when someone sneezes, because it is funny, and we say "That's really funny" when someone sneezes a second time. It can get pretty hilarious when the pollen comes out and gets blown around in the desert. "That's funny" started with my friends in high school loving to say "*gesundheit*" after anyone said "nephew" or "a shoe" (puns are important to nerds), but that left us with nothing to say after a sneeze. "That's funny" covered it. While other students were tagging cars, shooting dope, and reading literature, we were figuring out how to react properly to sneezes and words that sound like sneezes. In our children's preschool, our children have said "Bless you" a few times, but all the children there say "That's funny." Further support for Jefferson's conviction that good ideas would drive out bad ones in the marketplace of ideas.

We've tried to create a Jillette winter ritual around Xmas. We've chosen New Year's Day. Teller and I finally made enough money that we don't have to work New Year's Eve anymore. In showbiz it's about the most lucrative night of the year, but also the most depressing. Venues pay three times what they normally would for a show. Everyone in the audience gets a hat and a noisemaker, and no one gives a fuck about the show. Every year would end with a nice big check and a show that we hated doing, so we said fuck it, and now we take New Year's Eve off. As you know, I've never had a drink of alcohol or tried any recreational drug in my life. Neither did my parents. I was brought up to watch TV and eat ice cream on New Year's Eve and that's what I do with my children. I don't do a show on New Year's Day. On Thanksgiving, Fourth of July, Memorial Day, Mother's Day, Father's Day, Labor Day, and Xmas, I do shows, but New Year's Eve I'm with my family.

My mom died on New Year's Day. When she died, I was on a plane flying to a gig in Lake Tahoe. I landed to a message on my cell phone from my sister. "One voice mail message" was a death notice. I'd been at Mom's bedside with the morphine pump in my hand when she'd gone into a coma a few days before. Her dying wish was that I not miss any shows. She said that they had raised me to work hard and keep my commitments, and her dying was no excuse to negate the work ethic they'd tried to instill in me. So, I've done the trifecta. I did shows the night my dad died, the night my mom died, and the night my sister died.

When Gilbert Gottfried's mom died, he called me. My mom had died about a year earlier and I had called him and we had gone out to dinner. During our grief we got together and made jokes in worse taste than you've ever heard. Our movie *The Aristocrats* is nothing; I'm talking about jokes that if I even hinted at obliquely, you'd put this book down and start organizing boycotts. I know that you wouldn't be reading this book unless you were a freedom-of-speech extremist, so you wouldn't want us arrested, but you would want us to never work again. Gilbert and I did those jokes just to each other. Horrible, unfunny, gross, hateful jokes for hours and hours, just laughing and laughing at the pain and suffering of life. Sickening jokes. Just spewing out a "fuck you" to the whole world. Yes, I remembered all the wonderful times with my mom, and yes, I cried alone for hours, but I also told jokes with Gilbert I would never let anyone else in any situation hear me tell. Jokes that I had never told. It was a time for sadness and memory, and it was also a time for pure, raw, empty hate at the pain of life.

We had dinner and made the same jokes after Gilbert's mom died. A couple of days later Gilbert was booked to do *The Hollywood Squares.*

He said he couldn't think of a reason to do *The Hollywood Squares* after his mom had died. I said, "Yup, there's no reason. But there's never going to be a reason. Your mom will never be alive again. There will never be a reason to do *The Hollywood Squares* again. You knew your mom was going to die, so there was never a reason to do *The Hollywood Squares* before. There never was a reason and there never will be a reason to do *The Hollywood Squares,* except that that's what we do. We're fucking guys who do *The Hollywood Squares,* except now we're fucking guys with dead mothers who do *The Hollywood Squares.*" I think he went and did it, I don't know. I cared about his mom dying, but I don't care about the fucking *Hollywood Squares.* If he did it, he was funny, I will bet my life on that.

Gilbert had to think about it. He had to decide when to go back to work. My mom made it easy for me. She told me I'd miss her forever, and taking a night off wasn't going to help. She didn't give me a choice. When my dad died, my mom lied to me. She said he was still alive when I called her from backstage at a show in Concord, New Hampshire. She kept the news from me so I could do a show that night and not be ripped apart. My sister and nephews disagreed. They thought I had a right to know, but my mom didn't care. With no support from the family, she lied to me. She told me to hurry home to her right after the show, and I did. Friends drove me in a car for hours, and she was waiting up in her chair, crying. She told me when I got home and was with her that my father had died that afternoon. Fuck your Santa Claus in the neck; Valda Jillette loved me enough to lie to me about the death of the man she had loved her whole life. Match that with "Oh, the guy in the supermarket is one of his elves who dresses up like Santa," motherfucker.

I lied to my mom too. When my dad got really sick, he was in the hospital on Xmas Eve. The doctors said that Samuel H. Jillette was to start in a nursing home on Xmas day. The bullshit social worker told me she would tell him and it would be okay. She was a professional, paid by the county. She was a liberal. She told him, and dad began sobbing softly. Crying was not a big deal for my dad. He was enough of a man to cry at Hallmark commercials. If you did a cheesy TV show with a horse or a family in it, my dad would cry. He would cry and wipe his eyes, and my mom would throw something at him and call him a fool. My dad taught me to cry at everything, and my mom threw shit at both of us. He cried at TV, not at real life. He did, however, sob that day. He certainly wouldn't ever complain, but he wouldn't be happy with the nursing home. He wouldn't be happy away from his wife and the house they built themselves, just the two of them. But he felt he had no choice, so he sobbed.

My dad never took a penny from me. Country and western stars always buy their moms and dads houses when their first record hits, and when our Broadway show took off, I would have bought my mom and dad Dollywood, but they lived in that house they'd built together and I wasn't going to change that. When I had more money than god in the eighties (god wasn't doing well in the eighties), if I came home and we went out to dinner at the HoJo, my dad paid. If I'd reached for my wallet he would have been insulted. When I was forty years old and came home in a limo to go to the county fair, my dad gave me two bucks to buy a candied apple for myself. Nothing made him happier than his son taking money from him for a treat. My dad did not take money from me. I asked the social worker how my dad could stay home instead of going to a nursing home. She said he couldn't. She said he needed nursing care around the clock. I said, "I can afford for him to have that in his home." She said, "No home-care agency will ever start a new account tomorrow, on Xmas day." I said, "I can make them an offer that'll make it worth their while to start tomorrow." Then I told her I needed a humanitarian service from her: "I need you to go in there and tell my dad that there's a government program that will pay for him to have nursing care around the clock and he can stay home." Little Ms. Sensitive New England County Social Worker, with the short hair and sneakers, said she didn't lie and wouldn't lie for me. I told her she was going to lie for me. She said no. I said, "I'll make this simple. You go in that room and you lie to my dad and make him believe it, or I'm going to hit you as hard as I can. I've never hit anyone in my life, but I'm two hundred and eighty pounds and I'm pretty sure I can do some damage to an intense New England salt-and-pepper-haired social worker. You'll call the police and I'll go to jail, but I won't let you ruin our family without a fight." I don't know if I would have really hit her, but I knew I had to make sure she would be able to give me all the blame for the lie she was being forced to tell. Her conscience was clear and she could hate me forever. I'm okay with that.

Little Ms. Down Vest lied to my dad and he came home happy. On Xmas day the health care professionals, those astronaut heroes at a low wage, those wonder men and women (ours were all women) who care for people near the end of their lives, started working around the clock for the government—which, at that Jillette house, was me. Our Xmas dinner that year was cooked by me and a home-care person, and my dad was thankful, and my mom and dad lived at home until they died. On that first Xmas night, which was supposed to find my dad in the nursing home, my mom and I had a conversation. We had it right in the room with my dad. He didn't hear well and napped a lot, so we could talk behind his back in front of him.

My mom said, "I know very well the government isn't paying for all this. You're paying for this. You're paying for all this care. That woman lied to your father and me and she did it because you made her do it. You made her lie." I said, "Mom, if you say that louder, if you say that to Dad, he'll throw a fit and he'll be in a nursing home for the rest of his life, and soon you'll be there too. If you tell my father that I'm paying for this, your daughter—my dear sister—will be so sad to have to visit him in there, and things will be much harder for her. Mom, I love you and Dad. I love you enough to lie to you to allow you to stay in your home. So, Mom . . . I promise you . . . I give you my word that I'm not paying for a penny of this home care."

My mom looked at me with a tear in her eye, smiled a little, and said, "Well, if you give your word, I have to believe you; I know you would never lie to me."

"I never would, Mom. I love you."

And we grinned at each other.

I'm not above lying to people I love, but really . . . about a fat guy with toys? Let's save the fucking lies for when we really need them. I'm writing this in a coffee shop at an Indian casino a couple of hours out of Portland, Oregon. A very nice woman just asked me to pose for a picture with her daughter, who is in a wheelchair.

I told them, "Please forgive my eyes for being so red and runny . . . it's the allergies, I live in the desert and all this green really gets to my eyes." I didn't want to say "I'm crying my eyes out while I type into my iPad about my mom and dad dying to the sound of slot machines." I don't only lie only about important things, I lie about allergies and frozen yogurt when the truth would be better, but, fuck, the North Pole?

My mom went into a coma a few days before New Year's Day. While she was in her bedroom, which had been turned by the heroes of health care into a hospital room, with oxygen and morphine and magic beds to protect her paralyzed body from bedsores, she had helium balloons to watch. I don't remember who got them for her, it might have been me, but I think it was Teller—he's one balloon-sending motherfucker. He has those cocksucking balloon people on his speed dial. When my daughter, Mox, was in the hospital, there were plenty of balloons from Uncle Teller.

My mom couldn't move and she needed someone to feed her, but her mind was sharper than mine ever was or ever will be. I sat by her bedside when I wasn't doing shows and read *Moby Dick* to her. Not because it's her favorite book, but because it's my favorite book and she just wanted to hear my voice. She would watch those balloons. She watched them move in the air currents around her oxygen. Finally I put a couple of the Mylar balloons outside her window, so the cold winter Massachusetts air would whip them around. She watched those balloons for hours. In the night, they were ghostly bumping against the windows, and she watched them. What else can you do when you can't move and you're waiting to die?

My mom asked my sister and I if we'd do her a favor. "Now what?" I asked impatiently, to try to get a little laugh. She asked that after she died, we would let the balloons go and watch them go up into the air. "Set them free." My mom did not believe in an afterlife; she knew we couldn't pray for her, but her wishes were for me to do my show and for us to let the balloons go. She made me get on with my life, and she gave us a tradition. After the show in Tahoe, I flew back across the country and my sister and I met at our mom's house. We gathered the balloons from Mom's room and from outside. They were a bit old and funky and there wasn't a lot of helium left. We took them out into my mom and dad's yard, and in the middle of a cold winter's night, we let them go. They didn't have much lift, but the night was dark and the wind was swirling and it was moonless, so they went out of sight pretty quickly. My sister, named Valda like our mom, and I held each other and cried together.

I'm trying to make that a family tradition. Every New Year's since my mom died, I go alone to a supermarket and buy a bunch of balloons, about ten or so, usually all one color, usually blue. Since my wife has been with me, she's been part of letting the balloons go. Since my children have been around, I buy some extra balloons for them so they have them to play with for the rest of the day. I go outside with the balloons and I hold the balloons and I think of all the people that I love who have died. I cry. I let go of the balloons and I watch, through watery eyes, the big bunch of color fly into the sky; I watch them until they're a single dot, and then keep watching until the dot is no more. I've been doing this for eleven years, and now I'm also thinking about my sister and my brother-in-law and a bunch more friends; there's more to think about every year.

The first couple of years, our children just liked the balloons. One year they cried about the loss of the balloons. They didn't understand that I was crying about the loss of their "auntie." We pronounce that word the New England/African-American way, with the "aw" sound at the top. My children call my wife's sisters "ants." It's two different words and labels to my children. I think last year they started to understand a little that Daddy was crying about missing his sister and his own mommy and daddy.

My mom got me through her death by making me keep working. Friends of mine who have lost a parent don't know how to start their lives again. My mom forced me to start mine that same day. A lot of atheists have trouble figuring out how to mourn without god; my mom created the balloon tradition and focus for me. Ten years after her death, and she's still helping me. My mom never met my children. She had the joy of grandchildren and even a great-grandchild through my sister's kids, but my mom was forty-five when I was born, and I was fifty when Mox was born, so we skipped a generation or two there. Letting the balloons go on New Year's Day is a way for my mom to touch my children.

When my mom died, I was writing to Linda, my high school fuck buddy, about how hard it was. It was before I had children, and Linda wrote back that it would be easier if I could also look down. She explained that we look up at our parents and down at our children. When we're in the middle with our children below us, it's a little easier than when we're at the bottom just looking up with loss and sorrow.

Atheism was a real comfort to me when my parents and sister died. It feels like if I had a shred of religion it would have been impossible for me to take the pain. The idea that a powerful, vibrant, sharp woman like my mom was becoming paralyzed and dependent, that a woman who would never let anyone else even wash a dish in her house now had to be fed by people who were hired to tend to her, was horrible, unthinkable. Even when I called in showbiz favors to get neurosurgeons whom we'd done corporate shows for to look at my mom, there was no guess as to what was wrong with her. It was kinda sorta like muscular dystrophy, but it wasn't that. It was like a lot of awful things, but it wasn't exactly anything they knew about. She could breathe and talk and swallow, but she couldn't move her arms and then she couldn't move her legs. Understanding that suffering as random was hard for me, but I could never have understood suffering as part of an all-powerful god's "plan." If a god had planned that for my mom, I would have turned to Satan. There's no plan I'll get behind that includes that much suffering for anyone. Random suffering is at least comprehensible.

I'm willing for my mom and dad to live on in my memory and in parts of my DNA and the DNA of my children. I fancy I see my dad in my son's smile and part of my mom in his eyes. My daughter moves like

I've always thought my mom moved as a little girl. I know that I could be projecting, and that's fine with me. It's just another way to love above and below me.

Our family doesn't have god and we don't have Santa Claus. We shouldn't lie to our children about yogurt, but we shouldn't lie at all; still, I don't want to lie to my children about ungulates being able to fly and the kindness of strangers who reward and punish with gifts. If I want them to dig a fat old man with white hair and a beard, I can just stop dying my hair and my lap will be there for them 365 days a year.

Our family, with our goofy names and nutty rituals, watches the balloons fly into the sky and accepts that we'll never see them again. Emily and I explain that they'll never meet my mommy and daddy, and they'll never see Auntie again, but we all love them all. We love them very much.

Then we'll have a nice dinner and open a lot of presents—you know, just like Christmas.

My mom didn't tell us what to serve. We'll have to figure that out for ourselves.

"Here Comes Santa Claus"

—Bob Dylan

The Bible's Sixth Commandment

Thou shalt not kill.

When you tally up the deaths from the attack of September 11, 2001, don't ever forget the people who have been killed in the reaction to that. Human life is human life. And the death penalty is wrong.

ONE ATHEIST'S SIXTH SUGGESTION

Respect and protect all human life.
(Many believe that "Thou shalt not kill" only refers to people in the same tribe. I say it's all human life.)

Why I'm a Libertarian Nut Instead of Just a Nut

I don't speak for all libertarians any more than Sean Penn speaks for all Democrats. I'm not even sure my LP membership card is up to date. I've voted libertarian as long as I can remember, but I don't really remember much before the Clintons and Bushes made a lot of us bugnutty. When I go on Glenn Beck he calls me a libertarian, and when Jon Stewart makes fun of me he calls me libertarian. I think those are my only real credentials.

There are historical reasons and pragmatic reasons to be a libertarian, but there are historic and pragmatic reasons to be a Democrat, a Republican, or a Socialist. I don't know if everyone would be better off under a libertarian government. I don't know what would be best for anyone. I don't even know what's best for me. What makes me libertarian is I don't think anyone else really knows what's best for anyone. Take my uncertainty about what's best for me and multiply that by every combination of the over three hundred million people in the USA, and I have no idea what the government should do.

My argument for libertarianism is personal morality. I start with the Declaration of Independence: "Governments are instituted among men, deriving their just powers from the consent of the governed." So, our government does what they do with my consent. I know barely enough about Max Weber to type his name into Google, but it seems he's credited with the idea that the state has a monopoly on the legitimate use of physical force. I put those two ideas together and figure we all give our government the right to use force. So it's not okay for our government to use force in a situation where I personally wouldn't use force. If I'm not willing to kill a cute cow, I shouldn't eat steak. I don't have to kill Bessy right now with my bare hands, but I have to be willing to snuff her if I want to chow down on a T-bone. If it's not okay for me, it's not okay for a slaughterhouse. Asking someone else to do something immoral is immoral. If it's not okay for me to break David Blaine's hands to make less competition for my magic show, it's not okay for me to ask someone else to do so. Someone else doing your dirty work is still your dirty work.

If I had a gun, and I knew a murder was happening (we're talking hypothetical perfect knowledge here; I'm not asking you to believe that I personally could accurately tell a murder from aggressive CPR), I would use that gun to stop that murder. I might be too much of a coward to use a gun myself to stop murder or rape or robbery, but I think that use of a gun is justified. I'm even okay with using force to enforce voluntary contracts. I would use a gun to protect the other people who chose to live under this free system. If I were a hero, I would use a gun to stop another country from attacking us and taking away our freedoms. I would use a gun for defense, police, and courts. Well, well, I'll be hornswoggled, that's pretty much what the Founding Fathers came up with.

I love libraries. I spent a lot of time in the Greenfield Public Library when I was a child. I would give money to build a library. I would ask you to give money to build a library, but if for some reason you were crazy enough to think you had a better idea for your money than building my library, I wouldn't pull a gun on you. I wouldn't use a gun to build an art museum, to look at the wonders of the universe through a big telescope, or even to find a cure for cancer.

The fact that the majority wants something good does not give them the right to use force on the minority that doesn't want to pay for it. If you have to use a gun, it's not really a good idea. Democracy without respect for individual rights sucks. It's just ganging up on the weird kid, and I'm always the weird kid.

People try to argue that government isn't really force. You believe that? Try not paying your taxes. (This is only a thought experiment—suggesting someone not pay their taxes is probably a federal offense, and I'm a nut, but I'm not crazy.) When they come to get you for not paying your taxes, try not going to court. Guns will be drawn. Government is force—literally, not figuratively.

It's amazing to me how many people think that voting to have the government take money by force through taxes to give poor people money is compassion. Helping poor and suffering people is compassion. Voting for our government to use guns to give money to help poor and suffering people is immoral, self-righteous, bullying laziness. People need to be fed, medicated, educated, clothed, and sheltered, and if we're compassionate we'll help them, but you get no moral credit for forcing other people to do what you think is right. There is great joy in helping people, but no joy in doing it at gunpoint.

I'm a libertarian nut because I don't want my government to do anything in my name that I wouldn't do myself.

"Something in the Air"

—Thunderclap Newman

The Three Dogmas That Hurt Americans Most

Because I'm a libertarian nut, *Reason* magazine, the libertarian nut magazine, asked me to write this article for them about the three dogmas that I think hurt America most.

"God"—There is no god. Imagine how boss the right wing would be without the religion stuff making them bugnutty. Without god, even Glenn Beck isn't all that crazy.

"Most people are evil"—This one bugs me even more than the god one. It's the idea that "well, of course you and I would do the right thing, but we have to protect society from the bad people." Most people are good. One has to look long and hard for a truly bad person. Laws are needed to stop the rare bad people from doing bad things to other people, not for social engineering. The left often thinks they have a monopoly on compassion; they seem to think that everyone else, everyone with a slightly different political POV, would fuck over everyone else. Cynicism is bullshit. Imagine how groovy the left wing would be if they just trusted most people to take care of themselves and each other. Without cynicism, even Michael Moore isn't all that . . . oh, never mind.

"Ask not what your country can do for you, ask what you can do for your country"—The first half is perfect. Your country doesn't owe you jack shit; it's not supposed to take care of you or stop you from being unhappy or offended. Government should do nothing beyond protecting individual rights (and "rights" doesn't mean "anything that would be nice to have"). The second half of that quote is 180 degrees off—it's missing a "not." It should read "Ask not what you can do for your country." You don't need to do anything for your country—you do everything for yourself, your family, and other people. What made this a great country is individuals. It does not take a village. Love people, not government.

"Gimme Some Truth"

—John Lennon

Jamie Gillis: April 20, 1943–February 19, 2010

I don't remember where I first met Jamie Gillis. It was somewhere on the streets of New York City, but I don't remember exactly where. I saw that smile, that hair, those amazing eyes, and I was thrilled. I had walked by John Lennon on the streets of NYC, but I didn't talk to him; why ruin the illusion? But Jamie was worth the gamble. Jamie had been a hero of mine ever since I'd seen *New Wave Hookers*. I saw that movie correctly, in a theater in Times Square that smelled of Clorox. It didn't smell of Clorox because they cleaned it thoroughly, it smelled of Clorox because ejaculate is alkaline, and we associate that base smell with Clorox. Before the Internet, porno smelled of Clorox.

Everyone says the sex in *New Wave Hookers* is wonderful, but I don't remember any of the sex. I remember nothing but Jamie smiling and talking. I've seen some good actors and talkers, but Jamie was better than all of them; Jamie made me forget all the sex in a porn movie and remember only him. I really remembered only one speech. I really remembered only one line, but what a line. For the whole movie Jamie does an aggressively phony Japanese accent. Toward the end of the movie, he gives a speech about how he used to be a square and now he's changed and his life is free, sexy, brave, and good. He finishes this speech, which seems to be sincerely from Jamie's heart, and ends it with "And now I'm Japanese, so fuck off!"

I couldn't stop laughing. I was cheering while my fellow patrons were jacking off. I loved Jamie's perfect delivery. It was surreal and inspiring, like Bob Dylan. My head couldn't really figure what it meant, but my heart kept singing it. For weeks I was saying to everyone, "And now I'm Japanese, so fuck off!" It still inspires me. I still think it all the time and say it once in a while.

It wasn't too long after seeing *New Wave Hookers* that I saw Jamie on the street. Penn & Teller had just opened Off-Broadway, and when I saw Jamie, I realized if our show was really successful our theater could smell of Clorox. I went over and said, "You're Jamie Gillis, I'm such a big fan." I stuck my hand out. I didn't have the balls to say his line to him. I did not say "And now I'm Japanese, so fuck off!" Who is enough of an asshole to walk over to De Niro and say "Are you talking to me?" Who could have yelled "Stella" at Brando? I just shook Jamie's hand and said I was a huge fan. I said I loved him.

Jamie smiled. It seemed like he recognized me, and then he called me by name; he called me Penn. He had seen our show. He said, "You know, for every one hundred guys who recognize me, one really hot woman will come up to me. I don't care at all about the guys, but it's great to be recognized by a hot woman . . ." Then he paused, looked me in the eyes, and said, "I put you in the hot woman category." Wow. I think it might be the best compliment I've ever gotten.

Jamie and I became friends. I was always thrilled to be around him. I will miss him. The world was better with Jamie in it.

And now I'm Japanese, so fuck off!

"Turning Japanese"

—The Vapors

Penn's Bacon and a Kiss Airlines

Does any American like the TSA? Somebody must think that someone else thinks it keeps somebody safer, and that that imagined safety is worth the loss of freedom and dignity—but so far, I haven't met that person.

I want someone other than me to run the experiment of trying to get on an American airplane with the New Hampshire state slogan "Live Free or Die" written on a T-shirt. That specific statism might get you a full pat-down. That slogan in context is even heavier. It was a toast mailed by an ailing General John Stark to an anniversary reunion of the Battle of Bennington: "Live free or die: Death is not the worst of evils." Fuck yeah! Also try Patrick Henry's "Give me liberty or give me death" for your comfy travel wear. See how a real patriot would be treated nowadays. Patrick or John's slogan on a T-shirt will at least get your ball sack fondled by rubber gloves in a bad way. I used to believe it was theoretically impossible to get my ball sack fondled in a bad way, but a TSA worker in Hotlanta, Georgia, changed my mind on that.

The Penn & Teller Show started touring in 1975 with just Penn & Teller in a white Datsun 210 station wagon with a sign on the side that read ATLANTA CENTERS FOR DISEASE CONTROL AND PREVENTION—

SAMPLE TRANSPORT UNIT in an official typeface. Our car was never broken into. I would drive, Teller would navigate. And we would talk. During those endless conversations we thought up all the crazy shit that would become our career. Our whole show was in that car. We'd share Motel 6 rooms at night, and drive again the next day to the next show, and talk some more about crazy shit we might could get away with onstage. By 2001, *The Penn & Teller Show* had grown to require an eighteen-wheeler and driver. David Copperfield has four eighteen-wheelers for his show. Three of his trucks have a huge picture of Mr. Kotkin's magical eyes and magic voluptuous eyebrows and THE MAGIC OF DAVID COPPERFIELD written in a very magical typeface on both magical sides. Our dirty eighteen-wheeler says ROAD SHOWS on the side in a generic typeface. It looks like "Road Shows" is a brand of soup. We could have gotten it repainted with some disease-control logo, but we're too cheap. We bought it used from some bus and truck touring company, and it was already painted. It says the word "show," and we do at least claim that.

Typing "eighteen-wheeler" makes me feel really butch. It's so purely American. In England they call trucks "fully articulated lorries," which is another reason we kicked their asses in the Revolutionary War. When Teller and I did a show for Prince Charles, we got in a line to meet the big-eared cheese after the show. Some royal handler gave us instructions about how we were to greet the prince. I explained to His Majesty's official officious butt boy that I myself was an American, and I would greet Chuck exactly like I greet anyone else. I would be polite, but that was all he was getting out of this freedom fighter—real Americans don't kiss royal ass. I was much more excited about meeting Stephen Fry and Hugh Laurie anyway; those are asses I'll gladly kiss. Chuck was really nice, though. He said, "Oh, you're the fellow who runs over the other chap with the fully articulated lorry." He had seen me running over Teller with a trick truck in the truck trick on our first NBC TV special, and part of being English royalty is using "chap" and "fully articulated lorry" in one sentence to polite but classless Americans.

David Copperfield travels with four motor coaches and thirty-one people. In 2002, in addition to one fully articulated lorry, we had no buses and eight people, including the two of us, all flying from show to show. Our crew is made up of freedom fighters, and when airport security ramped up, there were altercations at every airport on every travel day. It seemed to be a different member of our crew every time, although Stewart, our tattooed, hippie, redneck, biker light man, did go off a bit quicker and more often than the rest of us. I was the last to crack, but I'd watched Stewart flip enough that I knew how to go crazy about the loss of our freedoms. You learn shit like that when you hire patriots.

I cracked at the Hartsfield-Jackson Atlanta International Airport, flying back from a corporate date with K. C. and the Sunshine Band. The woman TSA-hole asked me to turn down the top of my jeans so she could check the seam, and that's not the way, a-huh, a-huh, I like it—uh-uh, uh-uh. I said, "Fuck it," and undid my pants and dropped them. I learned at Ringling Brothers and Barnum & Bailey the Greatest Show on Earth Clown College that when in doubt, try a pants-drop. I was wearing underwear because we had another show that night and I like to have my suit slide smoothly over my . . . wait a minute, I don't have to explain to you why I was wearing fucking underwear—who the fuck are you? See, I get in a pissy mood thinking about the TSA. Anyway, I was wearing underwear, clean underwear, and not a tight shrink-wrapped banana hammock, but dignified boxers. Yes, I was showing her disrespect by dropping my pants, but I was wearing shorts—"little Houdini" was not escaping. Still, she got on the talkie and called the real po po while a couple of her fellow workers took me to a holding area. She said that I had flashed her and I would be arrested for indecent exposure.

I said, "Listen, baby, if I'd shown you my cock, you would have known it."

Surprisingly, this well-reasoned, classy argument didn't sway her. I thought about leaving my pants down, in passive limp resistance and also as exhibit A of my cock not showing, but I pulled them up so I wouldn't have to be penguin-walked to the corner. The real police officer was there quickly. I guess he didn't want to miss my cock hanging out, but by the time he got there our crew was in full militia mode. They had circled the wagons around their meat puppet. The TSA guys said I couldn't use my cell phone while waiting for the police, so I threw it to Stewart and told him to call my buddy Bob Corn-Revere from my speed dial list. Bob is a way heavy First Amendment attorney. Bob has argued in front of the Supreme Court for your right to say "fuck" wherever you want. I told Nate, our Director of Covert Activities, to call the ACLU in NYC and get Nadine Strossen, a friend of mine and at that time president of the "All Criminals Love Us," on his cell phone. I don't remember why I was so sure that my cock in boxer shorts at ATL airport security was a First Amendment issue, but it was clear to me at the time.

Maybe it's that I have the words "Respect, Freedom, Peace" tattooed on the side of my cock, which expands to "Congress shall make no law *respect*ing an establishment of religion, or prohibiting the free exercise thereof; or abridging the *freedom* of speech, or of the press; or the right of the people *peace*ably to assemble, and to petition the Government for a redress of grievances" when I think about Fredrick Douglass banging Susan B. Anthony like a Liberty Bell.

By the time the peace officer arrived on the scene, I was ready to insist that the police officer talk to "my attorneys." Yup, I was going to make a local Georgia police officer talk to Robert Corn-Revere and Nadine Strossen, and they were ready to defend me and/or my boxer-shorted cock. I was so fucking ready.

"I'm your worst nightmare. I have two of the top freedom-of-speech people in the world on the phone. I have some time off coming up. I have money. I have friends with money. I have access to the media, and freedom fighting is a hobby for me. So, c'mon, arrest me and we'll have fun."

"I'm not going to arrest you, Penn, the TSA woman overreacted. Let's get you to your plane."

"I'm going to fight this all the way."

At this point, the TSA-hole came over and started complaining to the police officer. He told her to shut up.

I continued: "I'm going to fight this. You've got trouble coming. I've got the president of the ACLU on the phone here, and—"

"It doesn't matter, I'm not going to take you anywhere but to your plane."

"But she had no right—"

"I don't care, I'm not arresting you."

I insisted on talking to my lawyers. "You can't make them arrest you just so you can say they have no right to arrest you," Bob explained patiently to his asshole buddy.

I argued with him: "But they had no right to detain me."

"And they're not detaining you," he explained as if talking to a four-year-old.

I was furious.

The police officer took me directly to my gate and put me on the plane before anyone else, and made sure I was comfortable. He offered to get me a drink. I was treated like Prince Charles. I was still mad and told him, "I want her name and badge number."

"Have a nice flight."

I kept arguing with Bob on my cell phone. Because of his supreme rhetorical skills, he was finally able to convince me that I couldn't force a police officer to arrest me and that dropping my pants was not going to get me my day in the Supreme Court to fight the pig power structure.

I'm still mad. I hate everything about the TSA. When Shakespeare has Hamlet mulling aloud whether to off himself or not, one of the things in the "not to be" category is "the insolence of office." The Bard was a genius for being able to write that as a good reason for suicide before someone in a blue uniform with a big condescending smile told him not to put his shoes in a gray bin. Shoes go directly on the belt, Ham.

Writer, producer, freedom fighter, director, and actor (he was Chainsaw in *Summer School*) Dean Cameron created Securityedition.com. It's a website that sells little playing-card-sized metal copies of the Bill of Rights, with the Fourth Amendment (search and seizure) highlighted. Once you've bought a copy, you're turned automatically into a freedom-fighting performance artist. The Security Edition Bill of Rights sets off the metal detector and you say to the guard, "Oh, here—take my rights." It doesn't accomplish anything. It slows you down and slows down all the innocent people around you. It's a petulant way of reminding yourself and everyone around you that y'all are giving up freedom for the illusion of safety. The Penn & Teller show sells the Security Edition Bill of Rights at our theater in Vegas. We'd like to find a way to buy back all the ones the TSA confiscates and resell them. That would be a little government stimulus package for Vegas's premier libertarian atheist magic duo.

Contrary to what you may have heard about my waving my boxer-clad cock at a TSA employee, I really got no beef with TSA employees. But I've heard more people bitch about TSA employees than the system itself. They complain that the workers are just stupid, minimum-wage incompetents. I stick up for the stupid, minimum-wage incompetents doing their jobs at the TSA. They're just hardworking men and women trying to make a living, but that doesn't mean I'll ever smile at the fucks or keep my pants on.

We now have a security class in this country, workers who do security theater, whom the privileged hire and then treat with disrespect. The privileged blame the workers and not the system. The people in charge hire desperate people at a low rate with low training so people can be inconvenienced enough to believe someone is doing something. Even the self-aggrandizing assholes who run the fucking Hollywood studios want to feel important. They put in security. They want to pretend some bullshit studio would be on al-Qaeda's celebrity A-list of targets. Al-Qaeda doesn't give a fuck about Hollywood. Al-Qaeda doesn't follow American pecking-order rules. They are terrorists; they don't follow any fucking rules. Fuck, they don't even follow that "always use a 'u' after a 'q'" rule in their goddamn name. I got their true labiovelar stop hanging. Fuq them in the neq.

To be dramatic, Hollywood hires some stupid minimum-wage incompetent to look at the ID of everyone who's driving on a studio lot to pitch. Anyone who could do an improvised explosive device could do comedy improvisation well enough to get a pitch meeting in Hollywood.

They wouldn't need to sneak on. I've seen our manager, whom we call Spicoli, get on the lot with just his health-club photo ID. There is no hyperbole there. Our manager Peter Golden, who is a sweet enough talker to keep a show called *Bullshit!* on the air for eight years, was also able to talk his way past security on a Hollywood lot and drove his black Porsche past the guard without a fucking driver's license.

Profiling is wrong. You have someone look at someone's face and judge them by that. It's not fair. Profiling is for assholes, so my idea is to make the assholes do it. Let the bad guys profile. Eliminate airport security. Let anyone walk on a plane with anything they want. Let people bring guns on a plane, let them bring knives, let them bring mace. Let the pilot's doors be fairly secure. You might not even need that; the people on the third plane on 9/11 took out the hijackers.

There are heroes everywhere, they just have to know what the deal is. On 9/11, everyone's view of what to do in a plane hijacking changed—and it changed fast. In the first and second plane, people cooperated. They thought it was the right thing to do. It had been the right thing to do in all hijackings before that day. By plane three, in just that short time (we even have the time stamp on learning), we all changed. On plane three the good people fought back. Most people are good, so let people have any weapons they want, and the bad people will always be outnumbered. Let everyone just walk on a plane. Planes are in the air, but they're not magic. A gunshot in a plane isn't a lot worse than a gunshot at a Starbucks. A small hole in the side of a plane sucking people out only happens in those cool James Bond movies like *Goldfinger*, with the window popping out. It's not real-world physics.

So let the fucking terrorists get on with weapons, and let them decide who they take out first. Let them profile to figure out who might have a gun. "Okay, there's the guy with the MIA/POW camo hat; you take him out first; I'll get the cowboy . . . but wait, maybe the old lady has a gun in her purse, and what about that nose-ring guy?" Profiling is bad, so make the bad guys do it, make them find every weapon in the hands of every good nut on the plane. And while they're looking around and chatting, that cowboy might be silently profiling their terrorist asses.

That's not even my best idea. Profiling from what people look like is bad. Profiling from what people do is fine. First, we make all security private. Let freedom ring. Let people decide with their wallets how much security they want. Let one airline do full-body scans, and let another airline do nothing. Let people decide how much risk their time and dignity is worth. Of course, it's not just the people on the plane taking the risk; those planes can be turned into bombs and flown into buildings where they can hurt people who didn't decide to take that risk. That's why we scramble fighter jets. Defense is the government's job; let them do it. If the people on Live Free and Die Easy Airlines can't overpower the bad people themselves, then the professional jackbooted sky thugs can blow them out of the sky. It's part of the risk of freedom.

In that free-market air travel environment, I would start my company: Penn's Bacon and a Kiss Airlines. At PB & KA, we don't care how you look or what you want to bring with you. All we care about is what you believe in your heart. Most terrorists nowadays come out of the Abrahamic religions. They're part of the Mediterranean death cults. To most of these crazies, eating pig is a bad thing, and to all of these psychos, homosexuality is a way bad thing. It stops you from getting into heaven. It stops you from the glorious afterlife of a martyr, partying with virgins or raisins (depending on the translation).

So at my airline, there would be no embarrassing time-wasting scans and put-downs. No profiling. But before you get on the plane, our lovely host and hostess would offer you a piece of bacon. Nice, fresh, piping-hot, crisp, glorious bacon. If you don't want to eat the bacon, you don't get on the airplane without a full strip-search. Eat the swine, or bend over and take the glove.

Once you eat the delicious bacon (I bet I can get a sponsor), you're almost done, just one more quick step. Our lovely host and hostess have their genitals bared. I'll design the crotchless uniforms. The goods are just hanging out there all pink and naked. After you've swallowed the meat of the filthy infidel pig, you then drop to your knees (we'll have kneeling pads; we'll get them cheap from all the Catholic churches that have gone out of business in Penn's utopia) and you just give each of the genitals a little kiss. You don't have to throat anyone. You don't have to stay down there forever until she cums. Just a little peck on a pecker and a snatch. Everyone has to kiss the prick and the pussy so no one can lie about his or her gender.

I don't know how the Koran feels about drag queens, but let's not take that chance. The Koran probably says that rug munching is wrong, but who cares? Kiss both, get it done, it'll be fun for all. No matter what gender you are, my airline will make you a disgusting homo in the eyes of god.

I'm a genius. It's a really cheap fix. I might get Trojans or a dental dam company to be a sponsor. Maybe Purell will create a special product. I bet I can get our host and hostess to work for free—hell, I'd do it for free . . . free bacon and kisses on my rat, I'm so there!

Don't give me shit about PB & KA being unsanitary. You think two hundred light little kisses on a freshly rubbered, Purelled cock and cunt is going to spread more diseases than all those athlete's-foot-ridden stockinged feet walking across the same filthy carpet? And don't tell me there's nothing wrong with being gay, that it's just not your preference. Don't say you don't want to act all homo just to get on an airplane. You don't have to listen to Madonna and wear flannel, you just have to give a polite little kiss. It's no worse than that California air kiss you have to do when you meet a press agent at the airport. I'm sure there's a terrorist argument that if you're licking stick and split in order to be a martyr, it's okay. I'm thinking that anyone who's crazy enough to kill himself for god isn't going to want the omniscient god to see him giving a little smooch down under. But who cares? Let's keep their psycho imams busy on that quandary for a few years, and when they decide you can still go to Allah after licking infidel weenie as long as you do it with hate in your heart, I'll start Penn's All-Naked Airlines, where no one takes anything on the plane. Nothing. The man next to you is your joystick and Game Boy.

"Come Fly with Me"

—Frank Sinatra

The Bible's Seventh Commandment

Thou shalt not commit adultery.

Doesn't mean you can't renegotiate.

ONE ATHEIST'S SEVENTH SUGGESTION

Keep your promises.
(If you can't be sexually exclusive to your spouse, don't make that deal.)

Pitching Bullshit While in Mourning

On the morning of what Richard Dawkins called "the faith-based initiative" of September 11, 2001, I was soaking in the bathtub reading some jazz music theory book. A friend of mine, who was working as a stripper at the time, came into the bathroom naked and said, "A plane flew into the World Trade Center." I was thinking about how likely a G was to follow a D-minor seventh chord and I said to her, "What's that got to do with jazz?" She left the bathroom and went alone to watch the nightmare on TV. I went back to reading for a few moments. I thought about jazz for a while longer, and then what she had said started to drift through the swinging eighth notes into my consciousness. I jumped out of the tub and joined the naked stripper and the rest of the world in horror.

Teller and I didn't happen to have any shows scheduled in the few days right after the attack, so I was just sitting around at home, dazed. Bob Dylan's album *"Love and Theft"* (with the quotes as part of the title—I don't know exactly what that means, but it means something heavy) was released on the day of the terrorist attack. I had started taking upright bass lessons right after my mom died on the first day of 2000, and I spent the middle weeks of that September practicing bebop bass until my fingers bled and listening to Bob Dylan. Dylan's album, written before we could imagine that kind of terrorism on American soil, addressed my mood and thoughts perfectly. Great poetry can do that.

When I watched the Twin Towers fall, I said aloud to my naked friend, "There go our civil liberties." A few months later I called George Carlin and we were chatting about America's reaction to the attack. I told him my thoughts. He excused himself, put down the phone, and went and got his journal. As the Twin Towers fell, he had written, "There go our civil rights." I was so proud to have had a similar thought at a similar time to a genius. We were sad to be right. To react to an attack on our freedom with less freedom seems so deeply un-American. What ever happened to Yankee Doodle Dandy and "fuck you in the fucking neck"?

Teller and I had no sense of how things had changed that September. We took a couple of religious jokes out of our show right after 9/11. For those shows, immediately after, we aspired to pure showbiz magic. We *wanted* to be greasy guys in tuxes torturing women in front of Mylar to small-dick rip-off white-boy Motown music. A few weeks later, a Broadway production asked us if we'd try to help pump up ticket sales by doing the narrator part in *The Rocky Horror Show* for a week. 9/11 made me want to do everything that religious folks hated. I wanted to dress up in fishnets and wear lipstick in a mockery of procreation. Teller and I took a bit from our old Broadway show where I made out with a showgirl while we both ate fire. We decided to do it together, two men, Penn and Teller, for *The Rocky Horror Show.* I was onstage in drag. If al-Qaeda hated homos, I wanted to be flaming, making out with another guy onstage in New Jack City.

Way before that September, Mark Wolper, producer and son of a producer, had come to us and asked us to host a skeptic TV show he wanted to produce. From the moment anyone had been willing to hear a pitch from us, Teller and I had been pitching us hosting a skeptical show. Wolper set up the pitches for Thursday, September 20. When everything ground to a halt in this country, we figured our pitches were canceled. But on September 15, we started hearing the glorious sound of airplanes flying over Vegas again. President Bush said we were supposed to go back to normal, and we figured that meant we should pitch our little show. The networks agreed, and our five pitches stayed as scheduled.

We flew from Vegas to L.A. I don't remember which pitch was which. Wolper had some people with him, and we had some agents and suits on our side of the table, and they all had a bunch of suits on theirs. Teller, Wolper, and a few others had worked on the pitch for the show, but I was the chirp. Because I do all the talking for Penn & Teller, people seem to think I do all the talking for everyone. Maybe it's me who thinks I do all the talking for everyone, but I was doing all the talking for these pitches. It was awkward. America had to get back to normal, but did that really include doing stupid TV shows? There had just been airplanes flown into buildings, and we were talking about doing jokes for money. The timing was right for a skeptical show; we had all seen what faith could do. It was time to stop all respect for faith. It made perfect sense to pitch a skeptical show then, but it didn't seem that way at the time. We now know that a lot of Americans saw 9/11 as more evidence of the dangerous stupidity of religion, but at the time the media was carrying on about people going to churches, and our fucking president was talking about Islam being all about peace. It was the perfect time to pitch skepticism, but it sure didn't feel like it.

The first few pitches, I was making apologies for our skeptic show. I peddled with my foot on the soft pedal. I said that the nut side always had passion and the science side always had facts, but although the scientists were correct, they were a little dull. I promised that we would bring the passion of the nuts to the side of truth. But I was also cynical. I argued that people might watch our show because they hated it. I claimed that many people who were watching John Edward's necro-psycho rip-off sleaze fest weren't believers. Some skeptics watched to argue with him or to marvel at what an amazing predatory asshole John was.

In the Beatles' first movie, *A Hard Day's Night,* George Harrison wanders into the wrong room and the secretary mistakes him for a boy auditioning as a sidekick to a pop TV star. The TV bigwigs think George is perfect. "Oh, you can come off it with us. You don't have to do the old adenoidal glottal stop and carry-on for our benefit." When the TV folk mention their TV star by name, George responds, "Oh, you mean that posh bird who gets everything wrong?" Later in the scene he explains, "Oh, yes, the lads frequently gather round the TV set to watch her for a giggle. Once we even all sat down and wrote these letters saying how gear she was and all that rubbish . . . She's a drag. A well-known drag. We turn the sound down on her and say rude things."

I talked about the George Harrison *Hard Day's Night* Principle, which I had made up, to explain that people would watch our show because they hated it, and that would be fine for ratings. The network shouldn't care if they turned the sound down and said rude things. I was cynical. I underestimated our show, our audience, and mankind in general. Most of the reaction to our skeptical TV show is positive (if you ignore a few death threats), but in those first pitches in September of 2001, I didn't know what the mood was. By the later pitches, I had gotten braver, I was more aggressive, I had said "fuck it."

At one network, we pitched to a team that included a man who had, at one time, been part of putting John Edward on the air. I said something not quite as clear as this: "I'm not psychic, but I'm going to make a prediction. This is not based on talking to the dead or any supernatural powers. This is a prediction based on experience and knowing what a fucking scumbag John Edward really is. Within a couple of months, John Edward will announce that he is planning a 'very special' TV special, probably primetime, probably this network, where he will talk to the dead of 9/11. I don't have any inside information on this, I'm just guessing, but it's a really good guess. When Edward does that, and the bile of rage and disgust fills the back of all our throats, we, on this side of the table, will sleep well at night, because we at least tried to tell the truth, but the people who've helped him spit in the face of the innocent dead on national TV might feel a little sweaty and creepy in the middle of the night." When you're selling something, it's good to be friendly and flattering to your potential customer.

I gave versions of that "rude, self-righteous bullshit" (in both senses) little speech a few times. The pitch to Showtime went the best, maybe because no one in that room had ever booked John Edward. Showtime ended up buying our show. They didn't buy it in any cynical "George Harrison *Hard Day's Night* Principle" way; they bought it for purer reasons than our pitch gave them credit for.

We considered naming our new show the name Houdini would have used, *Hokum.* Then we decided to use the modern version of that same idea: bullshit. That ensured that *Penn & Teller: Bullshit!* would never have a proper ad or billboard. Criss Angel had a jive show called *Mindfreak.* "Mindfreak" is not a word anyone has ever used, but Criss was smarter than us. He was smart enough to not call his show *Mindfuck.* If we were as smart as Criss, our show would be called *Bullsnot,* and we'd be jerking off into piles of money.

Shortly afterward, we started working on what became the longest-running show in Showtime history. John Edward did announce he was going to do a talking-to-the-dead-of-9/11 show. That idea got such a negative reaction that John never went through with it. I was right about how morally bankrupt and socially tone-deaf Edward is, but wrong about the amount of character that TV executives have. They have much more than none.

"Sweet Transvestite"

—The Rocky Horror Picture Show

The Bible's Eighth Commandment

Thou shalt not steal.

Mike Armstrong is a very funny man. He told me a story about seeing a couple in an Indian restaurant in NYC, flirting over samosas. The woman leaned in for a little kiss and her hair caught on fire. The man didn't know what to do and tried to throw water from his heavy restaurant glass on to her to put the fire out. His hands were greasy and the glass slipped out of his hand and hit her in the head while she continued to burn. I laughed and laughed and laughed. Mike told the story with perfect details. I felt like I was there. A few years later, I told the story as though I had been in the restaurant watching. A friend had to tell me it wasn't my story. I also don't feel good about all the Dylan bootlegs I have.

ONE ATHEIST'S EIGHTH SUGGESTION

Don't steal. (This includes magic tricks and jokes—you know who you are!)

Maybe That Thief Kreskin Will Sue Me This Time

The Amazing Kreskin is an "entertainer" who implies he is psychic and, as far as I can tell, just does cheesy magic tricks. At the beginning of the nineties, I wrote this letter to *The Skeptical Inquirer* about Kreskin's involvement with their Committee for the Scientific Investigation of Claims of the Paranormal.

Letters to the Editor
Skeptical Inquirer
3025 Palo Alto Dr. NE
Albuquerque, NM 87111

To the Editor:

In 1966, when I was 11, I saw Kreskin on a talk show pimping a game based on the "science" of Extra Sensory Perception. He did some card trick "experiments," and I was astounded (hey, I was 11). This appearance probably included a half-assed disclaimer, his usual letter-

not-the-spirit "truth" that kinda says it's not REALLY extra-sensory, but I didn't know he was doing tricks. He deliberately misled me.

I cringe at the memory of begging my parents to buy me the overpriced "Advanced Fine Edition" of Kreskin's ESP. For their hard-earned money, I got a pendulum (with cards marked "Finance," "Travel," "Career," and "Love"—this is science?), a board, some ESP cards, and a pamphlet—all junk. The pendulum moved (ideomotor effect, like Ouija boards) and the other stuff just didn't work. My parents sat with me many evenings and we tried to get some results. We were wasting our time.

After several weeks of disappointing "experiments," I stumbled across a book on "mentalism" (I think it was Dunninger) and realized Kreskin had duped me. I felt humiliated and betrayed. It wasn't until I was 18 that Teller, James Randi, and Martin Gardner restored my love of science. Since then, a good part of my career has been dedicated to making sure others are not bilked by scumbags like Kreskin.

Don't say that Kreskin brought me to skepticism. There are others who deserve that credit; Kreskin just stole money from my parents, and time and passion from me. I owe him no thanks.

I don't care if Kreskin is with CSICOP as an "expert" on hypnotism or because of his "charisma." If Kreskin does not answer for his "mentalism," I will find another outlet for my skepticism.

I made a promise to an eleven-year-old boy.

Sincerely,
Penn Jillette

What an asshole, huh?

I don't mean Kreskin, I mean me.

Soon after my letter was printed, I got a letter from Kreskin's lawyers saying that he was suing me for writing that he stole money from my parents.

My letter clearly doesn't mean that, but can you imagine how hard I got? This was before my parents got sick and before I had a family of my own to support. I was starring in a Broadway show, doing movies, TV, and radio, and I had money coming out my ass. I was itching to spend every penny I had on this legal battle. I was going to take the former George Kresge down to Chinatown. I was going to prove, in open court, that he'd stolen money and lots more from my parents and me by selling us his shitty little box of shit. I was ready. I couldn't wait. I've never done cocaine, champagne, ex-wives, or boats, so I would flush my money down this self-righteous rat hole.

I forwarded his lawyer's threatening letter to my showbiz lawyer, Elliot Brown, and I promised Elliot I would make *The New York Times* look like pikers for what they spent on *NYT v. Sullivan* in Alabama. *The New York Times* was just fighting for freedom of speech, the press, and civil rights; I was fighting to bring down a hack mind-reader. Elliot, who had a computer macro that changed his closing salutation on every letter from "Death to the Fascist Insect that Preys on the Life of the People" to "Very Truly Yours" right before he signed it, sent this to Kreskin's attorney.

Dear [Kreskin's lawyer]:

We are the attorneys for Penn Jillette. Your letter of April 9, 1992, to [our manager at the time] has been referred to us. Although your letter refers to Penn & Teller, Penn Jillette was the sole author of the letter to The Skeptical Inquirer.

We are of the firm conviction that the statement to which you refer in your letter is not actionable in the context of Mr. Jillette's letter.

In fact, any claim that the statement is actionable would, in our view, be a frivolous one.

If you would like to discuss this matter further, please do not hesitate to call.

Very truly yours,
Elliot H. Brown

It was a lot better with "Death to the Fascist Insect that Preys on the Life of the People" as the closing, but of course the threat was frivolous and Kreskin backed down right away. I was heartbroken. Elliot had to patiently explain to me that I couldn't force someone to sue me if he didn't want to, just like a few years later when Bob Corn-Revere would have to explain to me that I couldn't force someone to arrest me. A few hours later I did a National Public Radio show and hijacked my own interview to try to repeat the stuff I'd written about Kreskin. I was hoping he'd pretend to misunderstand again and we could go to court.

Unfortunately, I stayed well within my rights. Sadly, the *NYT* had already spent enough to protect my opinion. I guess that's good; I had money to care for my parents as their health declined and my children will have money for whatever recreational drugs are popular in ten years.

In 1994, Kreskin was booked at the Debbie Reynolds Hollywood Hotel in Las Vegas. I know Carrie Fisher a bit, and if I'd known earlier that Kreskin was going to be booked, I would have given her a jingle and tried to have her mother fire him, but he was on the marquee before I noticed.

I felt compelled to see Kreskin's show. Teller and I went with "Master Magician Lance Burton," a showgirl buddy of mine, juggler and *Bullshit!* writer Michael Goudeau, and Goudeau's date, a professional topless mechanical bull rider. We know how to live. The showgirl wasn't showing, the topless bull-rider was topped, and we were all sober and quiet. We also seemed to be the only ones who had bought tickets at full price.

We got seated in the showroom, and the show didn't start. When it got way past starting time and the show still hadn't started, Teller and I got up to go pee. When we came back from the men's room, an apologetic white-haired maître d' said, "You Mr. Penn and Teller? I've been told not to let you back in. I'm sure you guys understand, professionally."

We didn't understand, professionally, and we politely told him we'd paid for our tickets, we weren't disorderly, and we were going to see the show. We walked past him and sat down. He followed us to the table. "You're going to have to leave." He had been ordered to get us out of the showroom before the show would start.

We showed our AmEx receipts and said politely, "I think you should call Metro." (That's the cool way to say "police" in Vegas.) I was hard about going limp. I've always wanted to do the passive resistance thing and be dragged away by police. I asked Lance Burton to use his big old cell phone to call a news photographer. We could Photoshop the pictures to black and white and add in police dogs. We were willing to fight for our right to see a shitty show.

We sat and waited. No police and no show. There was no nervousness or anticipation in the showroom, just us and a handful of people who had been given complimentary tickets because they bought a buffet lunch or something. Finally, after longer than you'd wait for Guns N' Roses, the lights went down and Kreskin walked out onstage like a high school vice principal.

Wow. James Bond always has really cool, strong, smart villains. My nemesis was a thin, pathetic guy doing a matinee for six fully paid tickets, some twofers, and a bit of paper. I started to feel sorry for him. It had been twenty-eight years since my parents bought me his shitty toy that I didn't really need; maybe I could just get over it.

I had won on every front. I'd publicly trashed him every chance I'd gotten. He'd backed down from the lawsuit. We were playing a bigger room in Vegas, and we hadn't been thrown out of his shitty little show. As he walked out onstage I was ready to forgive him. If not for the first thing he said when he walked onstage, I bet I could have forgiven everything I saw in his shitty show that afternoon. I could have forgiven his boring card tricks done with incompetent sleight of hand; his name-dropping of Johnny Carson, David Letterman, Sammy Davis Jr., Regis Philbin, and Skitch Henderson; his clamming piano performances of "Feelings" and *Superman*'s "Can You Read My Mind?" I could have shrugged off his desperately explaining over and over again how famous he was and bragging about reciting the lyrics to "One Life to Live" with some pops orchestra, and continued my magnanimous feelings as he then recited the lyrics to "One Life to Live."

I would have been tested when the mind-reading section came. I think the trick he did was by that 1940s mentalist Dunninger, just right out of his books. Kreskin even ripped off Dunninger's weasel words about his tricks being done "by natural and scientific means" and saying "I am no fortune-teller." I'm sure he considers this a disclaimer, but it does lack the important sentence "I'm not using ESP, I'm just doing shitty fucking tricks!" To do his mind reading, he asked us to write down thoughts on little pieces of paper so he could sneak a look (he thought he fooled people by giving them his word that he really wasn't sneaking a look). Teller wrote on his piece of paper "Dunninger is rolling in his grave," and I wrote the question "How do you live with yourself?" on mine. Kreskin never got around to reading those thoughts in our minds. He guessed someone's phone number contained "702," the area code for Vegas . . . and he was wrong. Even with all this, and his hateful opening, we didn't disrupt the show. We didn't make a peep.

He didn't do many tricks, and no good ones. They were hack tricks that have been around forever, and he's been doing them forever, and the only astonishing thing was that he hadn't gotten better with all the repetition. He hadn't learned a thing. The jokes he told were awful and he insulted the audience for not laughing, pretending he was working over their heads. He said, "You'll find yourself waking up in the middle of the night laughing." I hate when performers blame their audiences for not getting jokes. But I could have forgiven all that, I suppose . . . if not for his opening.

He even used Dunninger's closing line: "To those who believe, no explanation is necessary; to those who do not, no explanation is possible."

Dunninger was a big swinging dick. You could admire Dunninger's bravado.

Kreskin is a fucking weasel. Kreskin ended by trying to force a standing ovation, and as the audience walked out, he pretended he got one. Everyone who didn't have their back to the stage was embarrassed.

I could have forgiven all that. I've grown some since I was eleven. I could be bigger than all that. But I couldn't be bigger than the first thing he said when he walked onstage.

I guess he felt he needed to explain why his show was starting so late. I guess he didn't want to say it was because he was trying to get Penn & Teller thrown out and they were going to be assholes and go all limp-Gandhi on his ass.

What he came up with will make it very hard for me to ever forgive him.

When he walked out onstage, he took a few deep breaths, pretended to have some trouble pulling himself together, and said the show had been delayed because . . . he had been on the phone awaiting news about the well-being of his sick mother . . . and . . .thank god, she was all right.

Maybe his mother really was sick and he was really waiting on a real phone. Maybe. It's possible, I guess. And it's possible that while he was worried sick about his elderly mother's health, he was putting her on hold and trying to get Penn & Teller thrown out of the Debbie Reynolds casino showroom. I suppose that's possible. I know what it's like to have a sick mother and worry about her. I know that all too well. But when I was on the phone worried about my mom, I wasn't thinking about having people thrown out of anywhere, I was thinking about my mom. It's also possible that it wasn't Kreskin himself who decided that we had to go. Maybe while he was seeing about his poor mom, some middle manager decided that having Penn & Teller thrown out would give the boss some solace.

It's also possible that Kreskin was lying. It's hard for me to believe that anyone could be scummy enough to lie about his mom's health, even this guy who ripped off my mom and dad with his shitty little "Advanced Fine Kreskin ESP Set" and made me hate science.

If Kreskin was lying onstage in Vegas about his mother being sick, fuck him in the neck.

I hope he sues me.

"Love Theme from Superman"

—London Symphony Orchestra

"Liar"

—The Sex Pistols

Nixon the Aristocrat

I'm the right age for Nixon. He was my bogeyman. When I was a rebellious child questioning authority, the president of the United States turned out to be, without question, a lying sack of shit. I argued with my dad about Nixon. As my hair flopped in my face and my eye makeup ran with passion, I insisted that President Nixon had authorized people to break into a psychiatrist's office and then used illegal means to cover up his illegal act. My moral righteousness was pure. There was no doubt showing in my voice or eyes as I accused Richard Nixon of crimes. My dad's automatic defense of any president of the United States of America didn't have a chance against my youth and fire.

How did a Greenfield, Massachusetts, failing public school student know for sure what illegal activities the leader of the free world was guilty of?

I didn't. Like a toddler, I was just testing boundaries. Could I go off half-cocked about the president of the United States of America and get away with it? Could I listen to Neil Young and Country Joe in my bedroom, watch the Smothers Brothers on TV, and read Abbie Hoffman, Jerry Rubin, and *The East Village Other,* and spout that paranoid shit back at my dad and be correct? The way that father/son story is supposed to go, no. I was supposed to be wrong. I was supposed to look back years later with my dad and giggle about how wrong I was. I was supposed to say, "You know, I really believed all that shit I was spouting," and Dad would say, "Yeah, and you were passionate about it too. You almost had me convinced."

That's the way it's supposed to go. I didn't know jack shit. It turned out I was right about Nixon, but only by random chance. The showboating angry young man is not supposed to be right about much.

When I say something crazy and hateful, I always want to be proved wrong. My dad couldn't see doubt in my eyes (that's my superpower under this yellow sun), but doubt was in my heart and my mind. I knew I was an ignorant young asshole, and I was waiting to be shown that the president was really a-okay. I'm still that way. When I sit on Fox, CNN, or MSNBC and spout my nonsense, I'm always waiting to be proven wrong. And I very often am. That's the way it should be. When I carry on about our liberties being eroded and the government taking away more and more of our freedoms, I want people to roll their eyes. I want to go into the next decade with egg on my face and more freedom in my pants.

In the eighties, Penn & Teller did the Letterman show a lot. I'm still very proud of a lot of those spots. We were good because Letterman and his staff were so great. One of the people we worked with (after the brilliant Morty) was Frank Gannon. Before coming to work with Letterman, Gannon had worked in the Nixon White House and, along with Diane Sawyer, had helped Nixon write *RN: The Memoirs of Richard Nixon.* He went from Nixon to Letterman. I talked a lot to Frank about Nixon. He even suggested that Nixon would meet me for lunch, but that lunch never happened. Nixon chose to die first. Frank talked about Nixon listening to rap music, which he really did. Nixon loved the way rappers used words. Nixon loved words. I listen to the "You won't have Nixon to kick around" press conference and now it sounds to me like Bob Dylan's angry, surreal press conference in *Don't Look Back.* Frank said Nixon was our smartest president, and I believe him. Frank didn't change my mind about Nixon, but he opened it. He brought in more information. Nixon was no longer just a psychotic bogeyman, he was starting to become a complicated genius. I was starting to get that wonderful feeling of being proved wrong. Nixon, the broken genius, listening to rap music as he died, disgraced and proud, started to be a person to me.

Nixon said, "I'm not a crook," and when his book came out, people protested with the slogan "Don't buy books by crooks." Frank had changed me. It was years after it came out, but I bought and read the massive book by the crook and it blew my mind. I learned so much from that book on Nixon. It changed me. Yup, Nixon did all those bad things, but the angry young asshole in Greenfield, Massachusetts, was wrong. Nixon was a monster, but not just a monster.

In the crook book, Nixon points out a bunch of factual and ethical mistakes that Woodward and Bernstein made in bringing down Nixon's presidency. Tricky Dick contends that the *Washington Post* boys made the same mistake Nixon himself made. They thought the end justified the means. They thought that getting Nixon out of the presidency was important enough that they had to bend some rules.

The end does not justify the means. Nixon learned that too late.

Since reading the book by the crook, I've thought about this point a lot. The ends never justify the means. We're all living only in the means and we don't ever get to see the real end. We don't get any big accounting of projects at the end of our lives. We just get our lives, day by day, minute by minute, and we have to be good. There's no punch line.

There are no ends, there are only means.

The supposed end that did not justify Woodward and Bernstein's supposed means was the president of the United States of America resigning on TV. I watched it live, brokenhearted. Other hippies cheered, but I so wanted to be wrong. I so wanted Nixon to be vindicated. Fuck, I want O. J. to be innocent. I wanted my hatred of Nixon to be a phase that I was going through. I didn't want it to be an awful event the world was going through. I wanted my dad to be right.

Years ago someone showed me a videotape of outtakes from the Nixon TV resignation speech. I saw it that one time years ago and it stayed it my head; it was another piece of the puzzle in my long-term relationship with Nixon. I just watched those outtakes again on YouTube. And I watched them again. And again. The bootleg starts several minutes before Nixon goes live on the air to resign from office. It's his last time addressing the American people as their president. The crew is finishing up with the set, the lighting, and the sound. The recording starts as Nixon walks in with his speech in hand. The speech he will use to resign as president of the United States of America. It's a heavy speech. It's a heavy room. A tech person gets out of the way so Nixon can sit down for the final tech tweaks before they go out live.

Nixon looks as the tech guy walks away and says with a big smile, "Hey, you're better looking than I am, why don't you stay here?" Nixon gives a little laugh and continues: "Blonds, they say, photograph better than brunettes. Is that true or not? You are blond, aren't you? Redhead?" Nixon is telling the young sound guy that America would rather see an attractive young man resigning than crazy old Nixon.

Nixon then tells the still photographer to stop shooting. "I'm afraid he'll catch me picking my nose," he says with a laugh. Everyone in the room knows that's the least of Nixon's worries. His worry is that the whole world will not end before he makes this speech.

Nixon is making jokes. I think about jokes a lot. Especially jokes that cross lines. I worked on a movie, *The Aristocrats,* where we explored how far you can go with comedy. There was no violence depicted in that movie, there was no nudity in that movie, but there was shocking, unspeakable obscenity. It was the greatest comedians of our time showing that they could be funny making jokes about rape, AIDS, racism, pederasty, and 9/11. The comedians are amazing. Creative machines with nerves of steel. We made a movie about my heroes. My friend Emery Emery was one of the editors on *The Aristocrats.* I sent Emery the Nixon outtakes link and Emery flipped out. Emery knew Nixon was crazy, but man, how could he be this crazy?

How crazy was Nixon at this point? Nixon, at this point, was bugnutty, crazier than Charlie Manson's shithouse rat, but I don't think the jokes are any evidence of that insanity. The jokes and smile are proof that even with all that crazy and evil living in him, Nixon was still a strong, brave, smart human being, more fit to be president of the United States than I will ever be. The ability to make jokes is self-control. The Massachusetts boy that I was would have seen Nixon's smile as pure psycho evil; the Las Vegas man that I am sees it as superhuman strength. I see it as the best of us.

Nixon was not fit to be president of the United States of America. He had done bad things, he had violated trusts, and he had gone batshit. But no one is fit to be president of the United States of America if he or she isn't able to make jokes in that room right before resigning. If you're going to make decisions that are life and death to hundreds of thousands of people, and life-changing to billions of people, you had better be able to joke with more crushing pressure on you than anyone else has ever felt. I was able to make little jokes at my mom's deathbed. I was able to do that, but I did it through choking sobs. I couldn't have made jokes in that Nixon TV resignation room. I would have been vomiting. I might have died rather than give that speech. I don't mean suicide. I mean my heart might have just exploded in my chest. I might have shit out my liver. I could not have made jokes. That may not be in the top ten thousand reasons I'll never be president, but it certainly is a sufficient reason for me not to be president.

I was right as a child. Nixon was a crook. He was the president. He was not above the law, he was not an aristocrat, he was an elected official who worked for us.

But, as an adult, I know that Nixon, as a comedian, was an Aristocrat.

"Young Americans"

—David Bowie

The Bible's Ninth Commandment

Thou shalt not lie.

If you were a man in a monogamous relationship with a woman, and you were fucking a guy on the side and your wife asked you, "Are you seeing another woman?" and you said, "No," and felt you were telling the truth, you are a liar as sure as if your name were Liar Liar Pantsaflame!

ONE ATHEIST'S NINTH SUGGESTION

Don't lie. (You know, unless you're doing magic tricks and it's part of your job. Does that make it okay for politicians too?)

In America, Noblesse Oblige Isn't Just for Noblemen

I was on *Larry King Live* with Seth MacFarlane, the *Family Guy* guy. I like him. I like the pleasant feelings in my iPhone pocket when I'm with him. It's the gentle vibration of women I know texting to remind me that, if I get a chance, I could give Seth their cell phone numbers.

MacFarlane is funny, smart, attractive, and filthy-dirty-corporation-richer than the god neither of us believes in. Besides being a funny rich guy, Seth is also a liberal, and some women dig that. He's a real Hollywood liberal. Larry King brought up the Tea Party on the show. Rachael Harris, the woman from *The Hangover*, was on the show with us, and she explained that Tea Party people were racists. When I asked her to elaborate, she couldn't think of a racist part of their platform (maybe partially because they don't have a platform). Most of them are white, though, and maybe that's what racism means now. Most of the Sierra Club is white, and most of Jon Stewart's audience is white, but those didn't come up.

Seth didn't jump on board with the racism thing. Seth's problem seemed to be that the Tea Party people were politically in favor of policies that Seth felt were against their own interests. This is a position I've heard others take before. Seth wasn't hating the Tea Party people, he really wanted what he thought was best for them. His heart was in the right place. What bothered him so about the Tea Party was that they didn't know what was best for their own damn selves. Seth is very talented and works hard, but he also seems to think he was lucky too. That seems reasonable. He had done well, and he didn't need his taxes any lower. He wanted to pay his share, and he thought his share could be even higher. The Tea Party was pushing for things that would help Seth his own damn self and that were bad for the average Tea Party member. Seth explained that if the Tea Party got their way, Seth would, his own damn self, keep even more damn money. That really bugged him. He couldn't dig that at all. How could these nuts possibly be pushing for things that weren't in their own immediate self-interest? The Tea Party people were trying to stop the government from doing things that were financially good for the Tea Party individuals themselves. Seth didn't want people who were much less well-off than he was pushing for things that were good for rich fucks like Seth. I understood that Seth thought that anyone pushing for something politically not in their own financial self-interest was stupid and/or manipulated by big corporate rich-fuck money. This was my understanding of his position; those aren't the words that he used. I might be unfairly lumping Seth in with other people I've heard talk about this. This is an argument I've heard a lot. It's an argument some liberals I know seem comfortable with.

Larry and Rachael were nodding. It seemed they'd heard this argument before, and it made sense to them.

What the fucking fuck?

Huh?

As I see it, any person making this argument is kind of bragging that his political position is so purely altruistic that it is against his own self-interest. He cares so much about other people, justice, and pure political ideology that he has the moral strength to argue for something that isn't in his self-interest. I've heard a lot of rich Hollywood people make that argument. They seem to be very proud of it.

On the other hand, if a . . . I guess the word would be "peasant," cares enough about other people, justice, and pure political ideology to argue for something that isn't in his or her puny ignorant best interest, he or she is a manipulated idiot.

The problem with this argument is it's a robot killer! It uses the claim that the speaker arguing against their own self-interest shows how strongly they believe that the other side shouldn't be arguing against their own self-interest. Let me break it down to this: "I'm arguing against my own self-interest in saying that no one should argue against his own self-interest." Arghhh!

The only way this makes sense is if you think that rich people can argue against their own self-interest, but less rich people can't. Seth, I love you, but this is the United States of America—one doesn't have to be rich to be guided by what one thinks is right. Morality can trump self-interest in good people of all classes. If it's good enough for you, it's good enough for them. Me, well, I'd like my position to be moral *and* in my self-interest—and I think those aren't that often mutually exclusive.

I, my own damn self, am not a Tea Party supporter. I disagree with them on social liberties, our overseas wars, Obama's birthplace, Sarah Palin, and the conspicuous absence of tea at their rallies. But I do believe if Seth dropped his fat wallet at a Tea Party rally, the person who picked it up would be very likely to give it back to him. And if one of the Tea Party people dropped his skinny wallet near Seth, Seth would give it back. It's not in either of their immediate self-interest, but it's the right thing to do. Seth and the Tea Party don't disagree on doing the right thing, they disagree on what the right thing is. I just wish we all could remember that.

And just for the record, the government doesn't stop you from paying more than you owe in taxes. If you really believe you should be paying more . . . just skip the deductions. I'm sure you can find a way to give 100 percent of your earnings to the government and not be arrested for anything . . . except vagrancy.

"Have a Cuppa Tea"

—The Kinks

Would This Seem Crazy If You Read It in a Book?

I was on the road for many years of my life. For years, I traveled most days of the week and did shows most nights. I was happy living in hotel rooms. I didn't have children, and I called my mom and dad every day. I loved having friends all over the country and seeing them every couple of years. It's really hard to have arguments with people you see only once every two years.

On the road, you get along with everyone. The same is true for "romantic relationships." The first couple of days are the easiest in a relationship, and the road keeps everyone at the first couple days. Nothing can follow you on the road.

There was a woman who worked at a theater that we played. She was so sexy. She had an amazing body. Great writers have written about sexual qualities, and I won't try to compete, but . . . this woman was sexy. Cartoon sexy. She looked as though a very talented sixteen-year-old boy with a hard-on (redundant) had sketched her body and it had become flesh.

As soon as I arrived, one of the local crew guys warned me she was "too crazy to fuck." Robbie Libbon, one of my best friends, who also works on our crew and helped me with this book, took one look at her and said, "Holy fuck, she's got to be weapons-grade crazy." I thought for a few seconds that I should take the advice of someone who knows and just stay away from her. That didn't last. Even in baggy clothes she was amazing, and she was smart and fun to talk to. She wrote sci-fi movies, and since way back then she's had one of her movies hit the big screen. She wasn't just perfect tits and a perfect ass. She was great in every way—smart, funny, cool. Yeah, you could kind of feel the crazy coming off her like stink, but how bad could it be?

We talked, and then we flirted, and then we hung out, and then we fucked. It didn't seem there was any head room above her sexiness in a sweater and jeans, but she was even sexier when the rubber hit the road. We had a blast. What a night.

Then she brought the crazy. It bloomed fast. I hadn't even gotten back to my room when there was a four-page fax (it was way back then) at the desk of the hotel. Handwritten, small, psycho R. Crumb's–brother writing, telling me about our future together and what I had to do now. She was making demands. She was halfway to "I will not be ignored" bunny boiling, and I had hardly even stopped fucking her. Oh, my word.

I decided to be honest. I'd never tried that with crazy before. After reading the fax, I called her up and asked her out to lunch. We went to a soul food restaurant, and over hot links, ribs, and pulled pork, I decided to just tell her the truth as I saw it:

"People think you're crazier than a shithouse rat. You are the sexiest woman I've ever seen. You told me last night that last Halloween you had a *Kill Bill* outfit that you filled out better than Uma and still no date. Do you realize how much fucking crazy that is? When I arrived in town, I was told where the closest Denny's was, and that you were too crazy to fuck. Those were the two pieces of information the local crew thought I needed. Do you understand that?"

She gave no reaction, but I kept trying. "How can I get you to understand this? Here we go. You read a lot. You see a lot of movies.

You watch TV. You write movie scripts and you've written short stories. I've brought this fax with me that you sent to my hotel. Imagine we're in a movie or a book. Imagine this is a story. Imagine you aren't you. You don't even know you. 'You' isn't even real. 'You' is a character in this story, okay? And this hack magician comes to town and fucks this incredibly sexy, hot, smart, cool woman. And when he gets back to his hotel, he finds this fax waiting for him."

I handed her the fax she had sent me that morning.

"So, you're reading the book, and then there's this fax from a woman that our hero has fucked once. He fucked her once! And you read this fax from her in the book, okay? Now, just reading the book, just trying to understand the book, would you think that the author wanted you to believe that the woman who sent the fax to the hack magician was crazy? You understand stories, right? You understand that there are people in stories whom the reader is supposed to think are crazy, right? You need to know certain characters are crazy to understand the book, right? And you know how authors let you know that you're supposed to think that a character is crazy? They make you think that with crazy shit the character writes, says, and does. So, you write this fax to me, and you're about to send it, and then you think, 'If I read this fax in a movie, would I think that the person who wrote this fax was supposed to be crazy?' And if the answer is yes, you just throw the fax away, you never send it, and no one knows you're fucking nuts. Okay?"

It seemed I was really onto something. I went on. "We all think crazy shit all the time. All our heads are full of crazy fucking whack-job shit, so before we say something, we just have to think to ourselves, 'If a character in a movie said what I'm about to say, would I think that character was supposed to be crazy?' And if the answer is yes, you just say something else. It's that easy. And then you won't be too crazy to fuck."

It didn't work. Even though I knew she was crazy, I fucked her a few more times, and she got crazier and crazier, and it didn't go well. It ended up very badly, but . . . I got to leave town.

A few days later I was sitting on the plane next to Robbie. I was pretty proud of the "If this would seem crazy if you read it in a book, don't say it" theory of living one's life.

Robbie listened to the whole story and said, "Penn, if you were reading a book, and one of the characters said exactly what you said to that poor incredibly hot woman, would you think the guy saying that was supposed to be crazy?"

"Brick House"

—Commodores

It's Not the Heat, It's the Stupidity

I repeat: "I fuck Jesus hard through the hand holes and cream on his crown of thorns." You say that in certain rooms and you'll piss some people off. I said it to a socially conservative Christian woman during a commercial break on *Politically Incorrect.* When we came back on the air, she was in pro-wrestling mode. She was in full flipped-out Andy Kaufman mode, attacking me like a nut. I had made sure that no one but her, not even Bill Maher, heard me say it, so she seemed really to have lost it for no reason. I had said my crazy thing quietly, off air, and her reaction was loud, on air. She looked like a fucked-up crackhead and I looked measured, tolerant, and sane. It was just a cheesy TV trick that you can pull on amateurs. Hey, what can I say, I'm a professional.

Talking about raping the pain of the son of god can get you a strong reaction, but nowhere near as strong as you can get from environmentalists without even trying. James Randi is a skeptic and is Penn & Teller's inspiration. Randi is our hero, our mentor, and our friend. The Amazing Randi taught us to use our fake magic powers for good. Psychics use tricks to lie to people; Randi uses tricks to tell the truth. About every year in Vegas, the James Randi Educational Foundation holds "The Amazing Meeting" and gathers as many like-thinking people as you can get from a group of people who want to question every time people think alike. They invite speakers as smart, famous, and groovy as Richard Dawkins, Christopher Hitchens, Trey Parker, and Matt Stone. We all fill up a big Vegas ballroom. There's lots of real science stuff with real scientists questioning things that a lot of people on TV take for granted, like ESP, UFOs, faith healing, and creationism. It's a party.

Every year Penn & Teller are honored to be invited. We don't wear our matching gray suits and Teller doesn't stay in his silent character. Teller chats up a storm. It's not a gig, it's hanging out with a thousand friends. A couple years ago, during our loose Q & A, someone asked us about global warming. Teller and I were both silent onstage for a bit too long, and then I said I didn't know. I elaborated on "I don't know" quite a bit. I said that Al Gore was an asshole (that's scientifically provable, right?), that I really wanted to doubt anything he was hyping, but when all was said and done, all I wanted to say was that I didn't know. I also emphasized that really smart friends, who knew a lot more than me, were convinced of "climate change" (marketers have changed the brand name from "global warming" to "climate change," having learned from Goldman Sachs that if you bet against yourself and have the government to bail you out with other people's money, you're golden). I ended my long-winded rambling (I most often have a silent partner) very clearly with "I don't know." I did that because . . . I don't know. Teller chimed in with something about Al Gore's selling of "indulgences" being bullshit and then said he didn't know either. P & T don't know jack shit about global warming; next question.

The next day I heard that one of the nonfamous, nongroovy nonscientists, Sharon Begley, had used me as an example of someone who lets his emotions make him believe things that are wrong. Okay. People who aren't used to public speaking get excited and go off half-cocked. Hell, I'm used to public speaking and I go off half-cocked even when I'm not excited. I live half-cocked. Cut her some slack.

Later I was asked about some *Newsweek* blog she wrote. Reading it bugged me more than hearing about it. She ends with: "But here was

Penn, a great friend to the skeptic community, basically saying, don't bother me with scientific evidence, I'm going to make up my mind about global warming based on my disdain for Al Gore . . . Which just goes to show, not even the most hard-nosed empiricists and skeptics are immune from the power of emotion to make us believe stupid things." Here is Penn, a great friend to your ass, basically saying, fuck you in the neck, Sharon.

Is there no ignorance allowed on this one subject? I took my children to see *WALL-E*. This wonderful family entertainment opens with the given that mankind destroyed Earth. You can't turn on the TV without seeing us hating ourselves for what we've done to the planet and preaching the end of the world. Maybe they're right, but is there no room for "maybe"? There's a lot of evidence, but GW contains a lot of complicated points that are moral and practical and cannot be answered by evidence.

To be fair (and it's always important to be fair when one is being mean-spirited, obscene, sanctimonious, and self-righteous), "I don't know" can be a very bad answer when it is disingenuous. You can't answer "I don't know if that happened" to the attempted genocide of the Jews in World War II. But the climate of the whole world is much more complicated. I'm not a scientist, and I haven't dedicated my life to studying weather. I'm trying to learn what I can, using the tools I have, and while I'm working on it, isn't it okay to say "I don't know"?

I mean, at least in front of a bunch of friendly skeptics?

I wrote a version of the above, in more L.A. *Times* language, for the L.A. *Times* right after it happened. The business with Sharon the cunt really bummed me. "Climate change" was a magic subject in Sharon's world. Was it a taboo in the skeptics' world, where I'd talked onstage about fucking Jesus, son of Mary, in all his holes and gotten a laugh, even from Christian skeptics? (Yup, there's such a thing as a Christian skeptic—ESP is too weird for them, but they're fine with zombie saviors.)

A year went by, and Penn & Teller were at the next TAM with The Amazing Randi, doing another Q & A, and we got asked the same fucking question. This is what I said this time:

"I tried saying before that I didn't know. And when you say you don't know, that's a jive answer, because if someone says 'Did the holocaust happen?' and you answer 'I don't know,' that's absolutely a lie. And I tried to say it about global warming. I tried honestly to say that I don't know without saying there isn't evidence there. I really sincerely don't know! It certainly seems like the evidence that— But you shouldn't be listening to me, I'm the least-qualified person to talk about this. This is why we haven't done a *Bullshit!* show about global warming—because we want to do stuff that we think there's a very good chance that we're correct about. And there is almost no chance we'd be correct about global warming.

"The only thing I'm trying to say is, if there is global warming, which there probably is, that doesn't necessarily mean we caused it.

"And if we caused it, which we probably did, it doesn't necessarily mean that we can stop it. Randi and I can take a tractor trailer to the top of a hill and put it in neutral, and we can start pushing it, but as it goes down the hill, we can't necessarily stop it just because we started it.

"So if people can stop it, which they probably can, that doesn't mean that the way to stop it is by stopping carbon emissions—which it probably is.

"And if it is happening, and we did start it, and we can stop it, and the way to do that is with carbon emissions, it does not necessarily mean that the answer is socialism.

"But it may very well be. I don't know, and I mean I really, deeply don't know. Not some skinhead Nazi 'I don't know about the holocaust' thing, but just really, *I don't fuckin' know!*"

I should talk about global warming only during commercial breaks.

"(Tropical) Heat Wave"

—James White and the Blacks

The Bible's Tenth Commandment

**Thou shalt not covet thy neighbor's house;
thou shalt not covet thy neighbor's wife,
or male or female slave, or ox, or donkey,
or anything that belongs to thy neighbor.**

"I just want to believe in god."

"I just want to believe I'm Bob Dylan, but it'll be healthier for both of us if we just live in this world the way it is."

ONE ATHEIST'S TENTH SUGGESTION

Don't waste too much time wishing, hoping, and being envious; it'll make you bugnutty. (Man oh man, that MILF at my child's school sure looks hot, but I have work to do.)

You Could Be Bruce Springsteen

You could never be Bob Dylan. You have no chance of that. You won't be Eddie Van Halen; you'll never practice enough. Even if you could write as well as Eminem, you don't have a thick enough skin to be him. Yeah, you can play bass as well as Sid Vicious ever did, right now, but you'll never be in that right of a place at that right of a time. You're already as good a musician as Ozzy or Courtney, but it's harder to be Ozzy and Courtney than it is to learn to do something. You'll never have the attitude required to be famous with no skill and no talent. You couldn't live with yourself if you stooped to doing impressions of people who really are talented, so that option is out the window. You're too old and/or not good enough looking to be in a boy or girl band. But, you know, you really could be Bruce Springsteen. You could be the Boss. Put on "Born in the USA" and give that a listen. It's a record you would have wanted to make. It sounds pretty good when you sing along, doesn't it? You could have done that. Anyone could be Bruce Springsteen.

It's not that Springsteen is incompetent. Not at all. He's not a hack. He's not sloppy. He's not a follower. Everything he does, he does well. He's a superstar and a major talent. And he's a superstar who's one of us. The goofy thing is that it doesn't matter very much who the "us" is in that sentence. Springsteen is one of the people, no matter who the people are.

If the greatest art conceals the art, Springsteen is a great artist. Sit around with your rock snob friends and talk about great guitar players, great singers, and great songwriters. Hendrix, Pete, Eddie, Prince, Page, Zappa, Clapton, Richards, and Carlos are some of the guitar names you'll throw around. Elvis, Lennon, Roy, Elvis, Freddie, and Fogerty are some of the singer names. Dylan, Prince, the Glimmer Twins, and Beck are some of your great songwriters. (There are no women on the list, because we're talking about "rock snobs," which is a boys' club. Yeah, lots of women should be on that list, but they're not; rock snobs, right now in this culture, are heterosexual men loving other men.) These lists were off the top of my head. I don't pretend they're up to date, complete, or even close to accurate—there are lots more in every category, and there's lots of room for argument—but the point is that Bruce isn't on any of those lists. However, if you're not talking to snobs—if you're talking to people who would put Elton and Billy Joel on that list—Bruce is near the top of all three of those lists. If you're talking to "the people," they'll pick Bruce right away.

When you go to see Dylan, you want to hang on his every word. You want to study how he stands, where he's looking, and how he breathes. Even when Bob touches your heart directly, there's still a lot of mystery. We're always studying Dylan; we want to learn as much as possible about who Dylan is. Dylan falls in love and gets his heart broken just like you, but Dylan isn't really just like you. Even when you mumble "right on" under your breath, even when you know exactly what the hell he's talking about, he's still Dylan and you're still just you.

You never get that feeling with Bruce. He's always talking about "us." Always. Even his personal little tape-recorded albums, done in the middle of the night in his house alone, are about us. He's even antisocial like everyone else. Going to see Dylan is like going to the most wonderful freak show ever devised. You're going to see "someone very special." He makes no attempt to reach you. You come to him; he doesn't reach out to you. Bob doesn't make you sing along. Bob doesn't ask you how you're feeling. You're there to see him, and his major job is to be Dylan, and he does that perfectly.

Going to see Bruce is going to a pep rally. When you go to see Bruce, you're going to hang out with all your peeps. He's a cheerleader for all our lives. I grew up in a dying factory town. I had friends come back from Vietnam. I had friends not come back from Vietnam. Bruce lets you sing along. If he had time, he'd get everyone onstage to sing into the mic with him. He's not on display; he's inclusive. He looks at everyone in the crowd. A Springsteen show is about us.

I remember seeing Elvis Costello for the first time and being bothered that people around me were singing along. These were private thoughts that Elvis and I shared. What right did these people have to sing them out loud? But with Bruce, it's "tramps like us" who were born to run. "We were born to run," not "I was born to run."

As brilliant as Dylan is, you can disagree with him and still love him and want to see him. "Hurricane" probably did it, and not everyone must get stoned. But do you ever really disagree with Springsteen? What's to disagree with? Where's he pushing the envelope? What creepy ideas does he have? He's not Eminem, dressing up like bin Laden and saying nasty things about sweet little girls with records out. Bruce has the same opinions you have. Yeah, he supposedly angered a few cops with "American Skin (41 Shots)," but I was at that show at Madison Square Garden, and as far as I can tell, the press was making it all up. People weren't walking out in disgust. They were walking out for hot dogs during a new song they didn't recognize. They just wanted to be fortified for the hits that would be coming up in the encore. It's a long show; you need provisions. How far out on a limb is it to say that maybe cops don't have to shoot the wrong guy forty-one times?

I remember a Springsteen line from one of the early bootlegs: "There's something about a pretty girl on a hot summer night that gets this boy excited." What?! What a creep, huh? Man, what kind of nut would get excited by a pretty girl on a hot summer night? That puts him out there with Ozzy, Trent, and Marilyn, huh?

I saw an ad for *Greetings from Asbury Park, NJ* when I was in high school in January of 1973. The ad was just the lyrics to "Blinded by the Light." That was enough for me. I bought the album the day it came out. I've been a Springsteen fan as long as possible without living in Jersey in 1970. I saw him live before anyone you know. I saw Bruce open for In Cold Blood and It's a Beautiful Day on May 6, 1973, in Amherst, Massachusetts. His hair was short and he was wearing a leather jacket and no bell-bottoms. Some of the hippies in the crowd (it was all hippies; it was an outdoor concert with It's a Beautiful Day) taunted him by yelling "Sha Na Na." The spotlight operators didn't know who to put the spot on. They seemed to think it was Garry Tallent, the bass player, and the E Street Band. This story should end with his blowing away the whole outdoor festival, but he didn't. He did okay. He did fine. He did his job. I left right after Bruce because I wasn't a hippie who wanted to see those other bands. I had hair down to my shoulders, and I'd never been to Jersey, but he was singing for me.

I wore out the *Greetings* record. I loved Bruce as kinda Bob Dylan, and I liked the next album, where he was kinda Van Morrison. *The Wild, the Innocent & the E Street Shuffle* is Springsteen's best album. I guess that's one thing that makes Springsteen different from everyone else. Everyone's second album sucks—even the Clash's second album isn't that good—but Springsteen's second album is the best in his career. I like it even more than any real Van Morrison record. It's amazing, it rocks, it swings, and it touches my heart. It kills me. And if you haven't heard it, you'd love it too. Anyone would like this album. That's Springsteen's style. You feel like you own his music.

On April 19, 1974, I saw him in a half-full little theater in New Jersey. This was so early in his career he couldn't even sell five hundred seats. Not even in Jersey. He did a perfect show. He had no less energy than when I saw him sold out at Madison Square Garden. So maybe that's a little harder than the rest of us would work for so few people. He's just like us, but he works a little harder. He's just like us, but a little better than us.

I saw the *Born to Run* show at the Guthrie Theater in Minneapolis on September 21, 1975. He was so much one of us that he didn't even stay onstage. Teller and I were in the front row and he ran into the audience and laid across our laps while someone else from the audience held his guitar. It was a great show. It made us dance around. Everyone in the audience was in his band. He was our Boss.

I saw one of his first stadium shows in Philly a couple years later, but with Springsteen, you stop bragging about the shows you saw after *Born to Run.* He lost me at *The River.* I liked some of the fraternity rockers on that album, and I bought *Nebraska* and *Born in the USA,* but when he was deep into his John Fogerty singing style and getting "Friends" to come up and dance with him onstage, well, I was too much of a rock snob for that. I loved him for appealing to everyone, but eventually, when he really did appeal to everyone, I started to lose interest.

But I didn't really turn on him. I never really trashed him. I didn't make fun of my friends who still loved him. I didn't argue. In my heart I knew he was still us at our best. I'd see the occasional video: "Brilliant Disguise (Makes Me Look Like Fred Flintstone)" and the walking-through-Philadelphia one. Okay, so I did make a little bit of fun of him. It's fun to kick people when they're up, but I never hated him. I never felt like he "sold out." No one can really sell out until they play here in Vegas.

Springsteen does play Vegas, and I still don't feel like he's sold out at all. It's always a great show. I saw him at Madison Square Garden a bunch of years ago. I hadn't seen him for a long while, and Max Weinberg invited me to go, and I figured what the hell? I went casually; I didn't really care. I'm embarrassed by that. It's a really jaded, stupid way to go to a concert. It's not fair to not care; it's not right. The tickets were really hard to get, and there are so many people who so want to be there; why would a person like me, who didn't care, take up space on that special night? But I went. And I sure didn't stay jaded for long. Damn, he was just as good as he ever was, and that's about as good as anyone gets.

It's hard to remember how good he is because he's so one of us. He's only special in being so good at not being special. He's not antisocial, outlaw rock and roll; he's good-guy rock and roll. He's everything that's good about all of us, rocking. As he sang, I screamed along with every lyric. I danced. I cried about friends and family whom I had lost. I cried about lost love. I was hopeful for future love. I danced for the whole show. I was crying and dancing. I agreed with every word he sang. I was really one with all those people at Madison Square Garden, and that's really amazing because I am a real creep. I have many deep political, social, moral, ethical, and stylistic differences with the people who were around me at the Springsteen concert. But Springsteen makes those differences unimportant. We were all born to run in the USA. We were all dancing in the dark. And we all wanted Rosalita to jump a little lighter. He can make me feel just like everyone else and like it.

And if Springsteen ever gets sick the night of his Vegas show and can't go on, well, we can all go onstage together and fill in for him.

Whatever you may be sure of, be sure of this:
that you are dreadfully like other people.

—James Russell Lowell, 1819–1891

"Seaside Bar Song"

—Bruce Springsteen

"Things Like This Don't Happen to Normal People": The Greatest Story Ever Told

Once upon a time, we moved from a very unsuccessful show in a tiny theater in L.A. to a very successful show Off-Broadway in NYC, and then to Broadway in NYC. We went from using our answering machine and handing out fliers ourselves to *People, Rolling Stone, The New York Times,* Letterman, and Stern. It happened pretty fast, and we didn't plan any of it.

One of the standard questions a Broadway performer gets asked is, "Is starring on Broadway a dream come true?" I never knew how to answer that question. I love doing our show, and Broadway is a fine place to do it, but it wasn't a dream. I don't know how people can dream of a venue. We know a magician in Vegas who always talks about how he dreamed of having a show in Vegas. It's the "a show" part that blows my mind. How do you dream of being in "a show"? All that matters is exactly *what* show. I didn't want to be on Broadway, I wanted to be doing that there show with Teller.

If you'd talked to Houdini, Sinatra, or Elvis, they would have all told you they should have been more famous. If you talk to Madonna, McCartney, or Stern, they'll tell you they should be more famous. And if you talk to Jay-Z or Gaga, they'll tell you they're going to be more famous. It's that dissatisfaction that drives them.

Teller and I are satisfied, and we were satisfied way before Broadway. The other Broadway press question we fucked up was "You went from struggling performers to huge overnight success—what was that like?" I disagreed with the question. We had huge success compared to what we expected or (and I suppose this is implied in the question) what we deserved, but we're not even the most famous magicians ever, not even the most famous magicians of our time, not even the most famous magicians to have performed on Broadway. We were the most famous magicians on Broadway for those specific years, but that's one of those "coldest Wednesday, June 17, in Greenfield, Massachusetts" weather records. We didn't really struggle. My dad was a jail guard and Teller's dad was a commercial artist. They struggled a lot more than we did. Teller and I spent a lot of time sharing a car and sharing rooms at many Motel 6s, but my dad had to put on a clip-on tie and work in a county jail filled with criminals. He loved his family enough to hate every minute of his work and never mention that to me until years after his retirement, and then only in passing. Teller and I were making more money than our dads ever had while doing the exact show we wanted to do. Our goal was to play for a couple hundred people at a time and make a living. We hit that goal fast. And then we passed it and it still shocks us. I didn't dream about being on Broadway; I dreamed of making a living doing exactly what I wanted, and you can cum during that fucking dream.

When Richard Frankel—the producer who put us Off-Broadway and on Broadway, and made us more successful than we ever imagined—first called me and told me he was a producer, I said, "A producer is a guy at a pay phone with a handful of quarters." We'd had lots of people bring us into theaters with plans for long successful runs, and it had never happened. The poor bastards would work their asses off and maybe break even and make a little jingle, but we'd never made anyone rich, so we'd never made ourselves rich.

Richard wanted to take us Off-Broadway, and we said sure. The contract we drew up (Teller and I did all the negotiations and contracts ourselves) was based on our expectations for another minimally successful engagement. It included a lot of stuff about getting minimum pay in advance and plane tickets home—and we made it very clear that we wouldn't help unload the truck, either.

At the time we traveled to NYC, I was living in L.A. with a dancer working as a bartender in a topless bar. For the purposes of this story, I'll call her Heather. That isn't her name, and she's not a dancer or a bartender now, and I've dated and lived with a few dancers and bartenders at topless bars, so no one knows who I'm writing about, and that's good, because she hates me more than life itself.

Heather and I didn't really plan on her going with me to NYC. We thought it would be just another gig, like Minnesota or Texas—do a few weeks of shows, break even, get our minimum, get some more confused reviews, and head home. Richard Frankel told us that NYC was a whole different thing, but people told us that about Texas. We'd been around the block and stopped off a few times.

Heather stayed in L.A., and I went to NYC. I guess things were okay with us when we left—I don't really remember—but we started growing apart as soon as I left. She was working as a bartender and I was talking about Stern and Letterman and *Saturday Night Live.* She thought it would stop the success from going to my head if she didn't act excited about any of that. I'm not sure that was her best move. As soon as I realized I was making it there and thus able to make it anywhere, I invited her to live with me in NYC, but she was dragging her feet. She still didn't believe my success. It was just her big stupid boyfriend and his creepy little business partner doing their stupid show. She came out to visit a couple of times, but things just got more and more awkward. She'd ride the subway and be freaked out at the pictures of me everywhere. This wasn't what she'd signed up for.

She called me from Southern California and broke up with me. I was sick of her and didn't care about her and was treating her shitty until the instant she broke up with me, and then, like most assholes, I was in love, and when I say I was in love, you best believe I was in love, L-U-V!

I begged her to get back together with me. I sent her gifts, called her nonstop, left her countless messages. No soap radio. She was moving on. I don't really know for sure what it was that made her want to split, but I think the answer is me.

I was sure that if I could just talk to her in person, I could win her back. Heather agreed to see me if I flew out, but said it wouldn't make a difference—she was done with me. I told Teller and our producers that I was going to fly to Los Angeles on a red-eye Sunday night and be back for the next show, on Wednesday. It was stupid, but I thought I was Benjamin in *The Graduate.* Heather had moved in with the person she knew who hated me the most, a lesbian friend of hers whom I'll call Mary. I'd barely met this Mary, but she hated me. Heather had rented Mary's guest room and could invite whomever she wanted, but Mary let her know she was against me and my desperate dickhead visit.

I arrived at the college-student-like full-of-hate apartment in the afternoon. Heather wouldn't change her schedule for me, so I had to wait until she got home. But Mary was there, and it would have been more pleasant if she'd just spit on me and kicked me. She insisted on sitting in the living room and scowling at me. I was so uncomfortable and afraid of her. Mary seemed capable of exploding my spleen just with rays of loathing.

When Heather got home, we went into her sparse little bedroom so we could talk alone. We sat on the single futon and had the very sad, sweet, hopeless, rote breakup talk. We talked until very late, and then Heather wanted to go to sleep. Although I could afford a hotel room at this point in my career, I hadn't booked one, and instead of renting a car I'd taken a cab from the airport. I guess I thought pathetic was going to be irresistible. Heather said I could sleep with her on her single futon, but we wouldn't have sex. I shouldn't touch her. Six feet seven inches tall, 275 pounds, in a single futon with her . . . just sleeping.

I couldn't sleep. I just lay there, uncomfortable, brokenhearted, on East Coast time, exhausted, not touching the woman whom I had convinced myself I loved, while she snored. Often when I can't sleep I take a bath and fall asleep in the bathtub. So I got up and tiptoed down the hall to the bathroom. I didn't want to wake Mary up.

This piece-of-shit apartment full of hate and sadness didn't have a tub, so I settled for a nice hot shower. I took a shower until the hot water started to run warm. I got out of the shower to find that there were no towels anywhere in the bathroom! I was cold, and wet, and there were no towels.

I poked my head into the hallway. There were two doors across the hall. One door might contain towels. The other door definitely contained Mary. I didn't know which was which. How much would a lesbian who hated me want a naked me to sneak open the door to her bedroom just to peek in? I got down on my hands and knees and looked under the bottom crack of the two doors to see which was her room and which might contain towels. I couldn't tell.

I went back from the hall into the bathroom, shivering. Then I saw Mary's blow-dryer. I hadn't ever used a blow-dryer (look at me, for Christ's sake), but I knew enough to know that blow-dryers blow warm air. Gambling that the noise of the blow-dryer would be enough like white noise to not wake up Mary, I turned it on. I turned all the switches on full. I pointed the warm air onto my body. It was the only comfort I'd experienced since Heather's breakup call.

The air made my chest feel warm and comfy. I bent over and blew desert breeze on my feet and between my toes. There was no banging on the door. The sound of the blow-dryer was constant; if I hadn't woken anyone by now, I wasn't going to. With nothing else to do in the middle of the night, I thought might as well get really dry. I dried my armpits. They were perfectly dry. The back of my neck. My back. My arms. So warm and dry.

I was the Louis Pasteur of hygiene. Fuck towels. From now on, after every bath and shower, I was going to use a blow-dryer. It was nothing like those bullshit gas station men's-room hand dryers; this blow-dryer could go where it needed to get the drying job done. I brought the blow-dryer around to my ass. It was time to dry my asshole. I spread my cheeks a little and man, that little winker was clean and dry. I picked up my cock and balls and did my perineum. I vowed that from then on, my taint would be as dry as the Mojave.

At this point, the blow-dryer had been on full for a very long time. I had been going over every square inch of my huge fucking body with this thing, and it was very very warmed up. Time to dry my balls. I stretched out all the little folds of my ball sack and brought the loving evaporation to my balls. Only one part of my body left. I was so embarrassed—before now, the bottom side of my cock had never been dry, not really. How disgusting is that? A little bit of shower water, missed by even the thirstiest towel, could fester there between the bottom of the cock and the sack. How could I have lived with that for all my filthy towel years? I'm telling you, that cocksucking cock was going to be dry, dry, dry. I was pure hygiene. I took the tippy tips of my fingers and held the tippy tip of my pee hole. I stretched my cock out and shot the blow-dryer straight up, the white-hot, burning blow-dryer pointing straight up as I held my cock by the very tippy tip of the pee hole. Blow, big man, blow!

All of a sudden there was a sound. Maybe it was the house settling, maybe it was my imagination, or maybe it was Mary, waking up to take a Penn-hating piss in the middle of the night. Maybe that sound was her, about to see Penn blow-drying his man's cock with her woman's blow dryer in her bathroom in the middle of the fucking night. The thought startled me.

I dropped my cock.

The tippy tip of the pee hole slipped out from between my highly skilled Broadway-sleight-of-hand-artist fingertips.

My cock fell into the blow-dryer.

Blow-dryer nozzles (at least this one, at least back then; I have not touched one since, I can't even look at them) have a recess and then they have a grate and then they have the white-hot heating element. I could try to brag that my limp cock was long enough to flop onto that grating, but it's not much of a brag; it's a couple inches, and I'd been stretching it out. The head of my cock hit the white-hot grating.

My cock stuck.

My dick burned onto the grating.

I had burning metal grating attached to the head of my penis, and I couldn't yell. If I yelled, then Mary would wake up, run into the bathroom, and catch me fucking her blow-dryer in the middle of the night. I don't know what I was scared of. What's worse than having one's cock stuck to a burning grate in the middle of the night in a two-bedroom apartment in L.A.? But I was scared silent.

I pulled on the blow-dryer and my cock just stretched out. The blow dryer and my cock were attached by seared cock flesh.

Finally I ripped the burning blow-dryer off my burning cock. Now I could smell it. I could smell burning cock in a blow-dryer. It smells a lot like hamburger, but not happy hamburger. Very sad hamburger. My cock was in shock. I was nauseated but still scared of Mary. I turned off the blow-dryer. I didn't want to look at my cock. I just stood there. I set the blow-dryer down on the counter. The blow-dryer giveth, the blow-dryer taketh away. I was no longer dry. I was now covered with flop sweat. There wasn't a part of me that wasn't moist. I don't know how long I stood there, but I finally looked at the head of my cock. It was like a Wendy's charbroiled hamburger with that painted-on, appetizing grid. It wasn't appetizing. I didn't know what to do. Boy Scouts hadn't prepared me for this. Finally I carefully put my underwear on and tried to pretend it didn't happen—even though I could still smell the cockburger. I opened the window to air the bathroom out like a guilty junior-high-school cigarette smoker.

The blow-dryer was cool by now. I couldn't imagine what would happen if lesbian Mary found pieces of Penn's cock in her blow-dryer. I looked into the end of the blow-dryer, and then reached in with my fingernail and cleaned the pieces of my grilled cock from the grating. I'm sure people have done things more sickening than that, but not in the United States of America. I put the blow-dryer back in place, carefully put my pants on over my underwear, and went out to sit in the living room and wait for the new day.

Mary got up first and went into the bathroom. I trembled as I heard her using the blow-dryer, but she got ready and left without a word.

Heather got up. She had slept well. She was in a good mood. She asked how long I'd been sitting there. I lied. She asked how I had slept. I lied. She asked if I wanted breakfast. I lied. She made us breakfast. I didn't have to go to the airport for a while, and she didn't have anything to do. We sat on the couch and talked. It wasn't breakup talk. It was friends talk. I forgot about the horror oozing in my pants. I even made a few jokes. Out of the blue, she leaned over and kissed me, a good kiss. Heather was sexy. Heather moved fast. She put her hand on my thigh and slid it over my jeans to my crotch. I grabbed her wrist. I uttered the worst sentence anyone has to say: "Um, before you do that, I have to tell you something."

Her hate level hit Mary's as she waited for what I would say next.

I'm a smooth talker. I earn my living talking. Teller once said that I "tell the truth well." I can spin. Heather was the first to hear "the blow-dryer story." She found neither charm nor sympathy. She said two hateful words: "Show me."

"No."

"Show me."

"No. I can't. I don't want to."

"Show me. Stand up, take off your pants, and show me."

"No."

"Show me your cock that you dropped in my lesbian roommate's blow-dryer."

I know that some people get off on sexual humiliation. I suggest they show their burned genitals to an ex-girlfriend. I've never experienced such humiliation, and I was the first one thrown off *Dancing with the Stars.* I dropped my pants and peeled the underwear off the blistered head of my penis. I stood there with her staring at my wounded, limp cock.

"Put your pants back on and get out of here."

"Hey, listen, we were doing well. It's not my fault. I didn't do it on purpose. It was just an accident."

"Things like this happen to you. Things like this don't happen to normal people. I want a normal life. Get out of here."

I put my pants on and went to LAX. I sat at the airport with my penis scabbing to my underpants. I flew back to NYC to continue being a star of stage, screen, and television.

Believe me, if I had had a cell phone with a camera back then, there would be the coolest picture in the world right fucking here!

"New York, New York"
—Frank Sinatra

Hello Dere

Marty Allen and Steve Rossi were on *The Ed Sullivan Show* forty-four times. They were also guests three of the four times the Beatles were on that show. They were a big comedy team back when there were comedy teams.

Comedy teams are out of fashion. The Smothers Brothers announced their retirement recently in Vegas, and during the announcement Tommy said that the only working comedy team he could think of was Penn & Teller. When *Entertainment Weekly* did their "Funniest People" list, they called our office to say we were going to lead their sidebar on top comedy teams. Then they called back and said they'd realized we'd be the only ones in a comedy team sidebar, so we'd go between Janeane Garofalo and Goldie Hawn on the big list.

When we were on Broadway, I got a phone call from an interviewer who had interviewed me before. She said, "I used to work for *People,* then I worked for *Us,* now I work for *Self.*" Yup.

Partnership got a bad rap. Friendship and loyalty started getting called "codependence." I love Ayn Rand as much as the next guy, and would have loved to have been the next guy if I'd been born a bit earlier, but sometimes you can be more of an individual as part of a team than alone.

In the fifties, comedy teams were everything. The biggest stars in the world at the time, and in the history of the United States, were Martin and Lewis. By just about any way you want to measure, Dino and Jerry were bigger in their day than Sinatra, Elvis, or the Beatles in theirs. Their crowds of fans stopped traffic when they were in New York City.

Teller and I have been working together for over thirty-five years. This partnership is the only serious job I've ever known. I met Teller when I was in high school, and we started working together right after. I guess Teller and I are friends. We were together around the deaths of our parents and the births of my children, but we don't really socialize. We see a movie and have dinner together without a business purpose maybe once or twice a year. I've been to Teller's house fewer than a dozen times in the past twenty years. We're business partners. It's like we own a dry cleaning business together. We're a pop-and-pop shop. We're not partners because we love each other or we're best friends; we're partners because we do better stuff together than we do alone. Our partnership is not monogamous—we do lots of stuff solo and with other people—but the stuff we do together is better. I really hope you like this book, but you know it would have been better if Teller helped me with it; he was busy doing Shakespeare, so you get me alone. Sorry.

In the nineties, Penn & Teller were playing Trump Plaza in Atlantic City. We were headlining. We were in the big room. I remember talking to Elvis Costello, Don Johnson (back in the *Miami Vice* days), and Billy Gibbons. The conversation was going well, and we talked about getting together the next day. None of us really thought we were going to, but we were being polite. Elvis said we should give him a call at the hotel and told us he was registered under the name of some famous forties crime writer. Don gave his checked-in name as that of a famous war hero. Billy Gibbons was registered under a famous nautical name. It was my turn, and I said I was registered "under the name Penn Jillette—Jillette with a 'J.' "

We were headlining the next night at Trump Plaza, and I was registered in my star suite as "Penn Jillette." The hotel room phone rang about noon and it was Steve Rossi. He introduced himself and said he and his partner, Marty, were playing in the lounge. I had never met him, but I was thrilled to hear his voice. At a casino, there are showrooms and there are lounges. Showrooms are theaters; they have seats and they're quiet except for the noise of the show itself. There's a bar, but it's out of the room. There are ushers and assigned seats. Lounges don't usually have walls; they are open to the casino, and you hear the jangle of slot machines and people talking and screaming while the show is going on. There are tables and a bar for people to drink at. When Louis Prima played the lounge, I'm sure all the attention in the whole casino was on his band, but for most entertainers, it's hard to feel like you're holding anyone's attention in a casino lounge.

Mr. Rossi was on the phone and he was inviting us to see Allen & Rossi in the Trump lounge that night, since we didn't open our own show until the next night.

I remembered watching Allen & Rossi with my mom and dad when I was a child. I saw them on Ed Sullivan with the Beatles. I was very excited. On a whim, I called Teller's room (he was registered under the name Teller, "like a bank clerk").

Teller wanted to join me for Allen & Rossi. This would be our social outing for that year. The crew was busy with load-in, so it was just the two of us. We met at the lounge, ordered our sodas, and sat at a table. Just the two of us, ready to watch a comedy team work.

There weren't many other people in the showroom. There was a TV on a wheeled cart on the stage next to the grand piano. It was showing A & R's greatest Sullivan appearances, Marty Allen with his fright wig hair (look who's talking) saying, "Hello dere!" Just as funny as you could be in black and white. I think Marty Allen's wife opened for them, singing standards to grand piano accompaniment. She sang well, and soon the clang and clatter of the slot machines left our consciousness and we were just watching a show.

Marty and Steve hit the stage. I think they had broken up about when the Beatles did and gotten together and quit a few times since then. There was some modern material, some Michael Jackson and

Viagra jokes here and there. Some new movie titles and busty starlet names were slugged in. Steve sang well and was the perfect straight man. Marty was funny. They committed like motherfuckers. They were working like they were on the most important show in television, with people still screaming from the Beatles. They were on and focused. They were great.

If you were doing a movie, this would have been a sad scene. Of the fewer than a couple dozen people in the lounge, some of them weren't even there for the show. The sound system was fighting to get over the casino noise. Some of these routines they had been doing the same way for forty years. They were still a great comedy team, but this wasn't the high point of their career. A couple of fucking magicians were playing the big room.

I looked over at Teller and watched him watch them. He was totally focused on their every word and move. He was watching Hendrix at Woodstock. He was watching the debut of the *Rite of Spring,* the opening of *Psycho.* He was there.

I once met Lisa Lampanelli for dinner before one of her headlining shows in Vegas. She said to me, "Now that I'm playing these big rooms and getting all this money and respect, I don't want to go back to the shit holes. I can't do it. I can't go back down. I just can't." I shrugged.

I was once talking to a Vegas headliner magician. He said to me, "Now that I've had theaters with my name on them, I can't go back to playing shit holes. I can't do it. I can't do it." I shrugged.

As I watched Teller at the Allen & Rossi show, there was a break in the action while people were applauding and laughing from the last bit and waiting for the next bit. Teller's attention wavered for a moment, and I saw him look around at the room with the few people, and the shabby stage, and the sound of the casino insulting the purity of the show. I pictured us coming out on that stage after a TV had shown us doing the cockroaches on Letterman and the upside-down bit on *SNL.* I leaned over and quietly said to Teller, "You know, this is us in a very few years."

Teller looked around the room. He took it all in again, doing a slow pan like a movie showing that our heroes were now playing the toilets.

He looked over at me and smiled a big smile and said, "I am so okay with that."

I began crying just a little, with happiness. Teller is my business partner, we work together, we're just two guys working together to make a buck.

But, in that smile and that sentence, I loved him so much.

"More"

—Steve Rossi

· AFTERWORD ·

Atheism Is the Only Real Hope Against Terrorism: There Is No God (but Allah)

The enemy is not Muslims. Muslims are people. The enemy is not people. People are good. The enemy is not Islam. The enemy is not god. There is no god.

The enemy is faith. Love and respect all people; hate and destroy all faith.

What the fuck was George W. Bush talking about when he said:

The English translation is not as eloquent as the original Arabic, but let me quote from the Koran itself: "In the long run, evil in the extreme will be the end of those who do evil. For that they rejected the signs of Allah and held them up to ridicule." The face of terror is not the true faith of Islam. That's not what Islam is all about. Islam is peace. These terrorists don't represent peace. They represent evil and war.

W certainly knows more about Islam than I do. What the fuck do I know about Islam? I don't know jack shit. One of my fleeting goals a few years ago was to learn to read Arabic well enough to read the real Koran, but I decided to learn to bow Bach on my upright bass instead.

Maybe I'll learn Arabic next year and see if I can get added to a few more watch lists. I won't change my name to Cat Stevens or anything, but just chatting on the iPhone in Arabic might get me flagged faster than a squishy bomb in my panties and my dad ratting me out.

I didn't learn Arabic, and I haven't read the Koran, not even in English. I've read the Bible three times cover to nutty cover, but I've barely thumbed through the Koran at the Vegas Barnes & Noble. I have no idea what's in it. I have no reason to attack Muslims. I don't know anything about the revealed wisdom or even the culture. I have no beef (or pork) with any Muslims. None. Muslims are people.

I have been to Egypt. Teller and I shot some TV show there. Our hotel in Cairo had "This way to Mecca" arrow stickers on the dressers to point everyone in the right direction for prayer. Teller's room was directly below mine and the same size and shape, but someone had moved his dresser to the perpendicular wall. The sticker had not been reaimed, so if Teller had trusted the sticker, his *salah* would have pointed the wrong way. Remember, it wasn't us that moved the dresser. We were in the Middle East; we were scared to monkey with anything.

In the USA, I'm an asshole, and that can get some idiots writing angry letters. So what? I'm committed to my beliefs deeply enough to have an assistant read some angry letters written in crayon, but I'm not committed enough to actually risk anything. Calling Mother Teresa "Motherfucking Teresa" on TV in the USA wasn't a big deal. It just got one more dipshit in his garage somewhere who calls himself Catholic even after his divorce, and claims by his lonesome to be a "league," to take offense. He wrote a few threatening letters and added me to his thinly veiled death-wish list with Bill Maher, Sarah Silverman, and Trey Parker on his FrontPage–produced, Geocities-hosted cheesy website. Matt Stone and Teller weren't on his hate list. Catholic boy was too stupid to realize that the partner who doesn't do the specific voice might still do some writing. Saying "Motherfucking Teresa" a zillion times on TV got me less flack than giving my daughter the middle name "CrimeFighter." I think that shows you how much serious power religion in the USA has nowadays.

But we're careful with Muslims. Again: Christopher Hitchens said, "There are no atheist martyrs." That's good thinking. If Penn & Teller were ever going to seriously punk a religion, we'd pick the Amish. Fuck them all and the nonviolent horse and buggy they rode in on.

In Egypt, loudspeakers would call people to prayer while we were trying to shoot our stupid TV show, and every time I heard the English translation of the Shahada, "There is no god but Allah," I would hear the first four words and think it was great. I really agreed with the first four words, "There is no god . . ." Man, I am so down with that. Agreeing with two-thirds of something religious is a personal best for me. In "Jesus died for our sins," there's nothing I agree with. I'm not sure Jesus ever lived. I don't believe dying helps anything, and I'm not down with the idea of sin. I'm not even happy with "for" or "our," those jive little pissant words. There's nothing in Jesus for me.

Of the 1,200,000,000 Muslims in the world today, about 1,200,000,000 of them are good people who will never hurt anyone. The overwhelming majority of Muslims are good because the overwhelming majority of people are good. But of the terrorists who have attacked the USA recently, a lot of them were followers of Islam. George W. Bush and Obama have to say how it's just a few bad Muslim apples, and that's just true. The number of Muslim bad guys attacking the USA is very low, but the Muslim percentage of terrorists attacking the USA is pretty high. Even if you call the antiabortion murderers and PETA whack jobs terrorists, the Muslims still have a high percentage. The 9/11 guys, they were followers of Islam. The would-be shoe bomber was and is a follower of Islam. The (would-be in one sense, and actually in another sense) dick bomber was and is a follower of Islam, and is still a dick. The Fort Hood guy was Muslim, but a lot of people seem to want to say he "went postal" instead of "he went Islam." Being a letter carrier is a job; Islam is a faith. Any job deserves respect; faith does not.

It's not fair to blame all the Muslims for the horrible acts of a few people. That's wrong. You cannot blame all those people. And we shouldn't blame a particular faith for the horrible acts of a few people. At least we shouldn't blame just Islam. We should blame all faiths. We should blame faith in general. But Bush and Obama couldn't do that. No religious person can do that. Being religious means being okay with believing in things without evidence. That's the most important part of any faith. Catholics say that questioning is bad; Jews say questioning is good; but they all say that faith is a-okay. They have to. The deal religious folks make with each other is: we'll argue about the specifics of our separate bugnutty crazy, but the general idea of being bugnutty crazy is good. Once you've condoned faith in general, you've condoned any crazy shit done because of faith.

The only people who can really speak out against religious terrorists are atheists. We're the only ones who can say, "We don't respect crazy shit that you believe." If someone believes they have the intellectual and moral right to believe that there is a positive force in the universe that watches over us and created us, well, that's not just the camel's nose under the tent on a slippery slope, it's the whole camel on roller skates living in your kitchen.

If you can say that you believe something just because you feel it, what do you say to Charlie Manson? Are you going to attack Charlie Manson for not being faithful enough? Look in those crazy eyes, just south of the crazy swastika carved into the crazy skin of his crazy forehead. There's some real faith in there. There are things that Charlie Manson takes on faith. And how is that faith different? Is the argument against Charlie that not enough people share his faith? Of course it's not true that the Beatles were sending Chuck messages to kill those people, but Charlie sure had faith that they were. If you assert that you believe shit you can't prove because you feel it, don't you have to give everyone that right? I'm not just talking about obvious crazy shit like virgin birth, arks full of critters, and seas parting. I'm talking about any kind of faith.

If you believe that your warm, snuggly feeling about the universe means a god . . . then Charlie Manson can tell you that those people were killed because the Beatles told Charlie about an impending race war.

We all act on things we can't prove. Einstein had to imagine $E = MC^2$ before he had all the evidence. That's different than faith. There's a humility to just imagining. There is a world of safety in doubt. The respect for faith, the celebration of faith, is dangerous. It's faith itself that's wrong. I deny terrorists the moral right to have faith in a god that will reward them for killing people with airplanes. That means I have to deny Christians the moral right to a faith that Jesus Christ died for their sins. That means I have to deny the warm, fuzzy faith that there's some positive conscious energy guiding the universe. That means I have to get pissed off when Luke Skywalker trusts "the force."

The only real argument against religious terrorism is to try to share the reality of the world. The world is plenty. We have each other. We have love. We have family. We have art. We have time. We have an impossible universe full of awe and wonder. We have an infinite number of questions we can work on. We have all the glory that is real and is us. We must stop glorifying faith.

Fuck faith.

ACKNOWLEDGMENTS

Thanks to my editors, Kerri Kolen and Sarah Hochman, who kicked it off, and all the cats and kitties at S&S. Thanks to my agent, Steve Fisher, who made the deals. Thanks to my good buddy Robbie Libbon for reading this over and over and giving suggestions. Thanks to Glenn Alai, who runs all of Penn & Teller and all the subsets, and who got the idea for me to do this book. Thanks to Peter Golden and Spicoli; they're both great. Thanks to everyone who is mentioned in the book, for giving me these stories and being part of my life. Thanks, Teller. And, of course,

EZ

Mox

Zz

I don't need to pretend to have god's love when my wife and children give me all the real love in the world minus zero, no limit.